ALL

I AM

IS

LOVE

*Awakening Journey
with Divine Poetry and Quotes of Wisdom*

Svava Kristin Love

All I Am Is Love
Awakening Journey
with Divine Poetry and Quotes of Wisdom
by Svava Kristin Love
ISBN: 978-1-942253-60-0

Copyright © 2023
Living Miracles Publications
All rights reserved.

No parts of this book may be reproduced or transmitted in any form or by any means, electronic or mechanical, including photocopying, recording or by any information storage and retrieval system, without written permission from the author, except for the inclusion of brief quotations in a review.
First Edition 2023

Living Miracles Publications
12365 Sams Wash Rd
Box 8812 HCR 063
Duchesne, UT 84021
USA

publishing@livingmiraclescenter.org
livingmiracles.org

Living Miracles

CONTENTS

ENDORSEMENTS 1
ABOUT THE AUTHOR 3
DEDICATION 4
ACKNOWLEDGMENTS 5
INTRODUCTION 6

PART 1, POETRY 10
1. HAPPINESS 11
A TRUE STORY 13
THE HAPPY DREAM 14
THIS MOMENT OF JOY! 15
A RELATIONSHIP JOURNEY 16
NOTHING HAPPENS BY ACCIDENT 18
JOYFUL LOVE 19
ETERNAL FRIEND 20
SOFT RELEASE 21
THE SOUND OF HEAVEN 22
DANCING WITH GOD 24
A TRUE LOVE SONG 25
BEGIN ANEW 26
GRATITUDE 27

BORN TO FLY 29

A GLORIOUS MELT 30

THE BREATH OF MY SOUL 31

YOU SPEAK TO ME IN SYMBOLS 32

IF GOD WOULD ASK 34

2. MYSTICAL LIFE 35

A CUP OF WONDER 37

THE ANGEL 39

FALLING FILTERS 40

LIQUID LOVE 42

A HEAVENLY TUNE 43

RETURNING TO PEACE 44

THE DIVINE BEING 45

CERTAINTY 46

A TRUE REFLECTION 48

CLUELESSNESS 49

CONSISTENCY 51

THE MYSTICAL PLACE 52

A BEAUTIFUL DREAM 53

MY LIFE 54

UNCONDITIONAL LOVE 55

YOU ARE WHAT I AM 56

WHO AM I? 57

LOVE AND BLESSINGS 58

3. TRANSFORMATION 59

- THANKFULNESS 61
- THE CHOICE 62
- STILLNESS 64
- ASCENSION 65
- TRUST 66
- TRANSFORMATION 67
- THE KIND VOICE 68
- STARING AT THE OCEAN 69
- AWAKENING 70
- KNOWING YOU 71
- THE ULTIMATE QUESTION 72
- WHY I CAME 73
- YOUR BEAUTY 74
- BELOVED ONE 76
- YOUR PURPOSE 78
- ARISE SOUL, ARISE! 79
- NOW 80
- WHAT IS REAL? 81
- BEYOND THE BODY 82
- LET GOD SHOW YOU THE WAY 83

4. LOVE & LIGHT 84

- A HOLY MOMENT 86
- DANCE WITH THE STARS 87

THE SONG OF THE LIGHT 88

UNDEFINED ONENESS 89

HOW TO KNOW TRUE LOVE 90

UNION 91

HOLY MOTHER 92

CALLING YOU 93

ONE HEART 94

THE LIGHT HAS COME 95

INFINITE BLISS 96

TRUE LONGING 97

ENTERING THE LIGHT 99

LOVE AND FEAR 100

AND SO IT IS 101

LOST IN LOVE 102

LOVE IS 103

I SEE YOU 104

5. GRACE 105

UNEXPLAINABLE PERFECTION 107

THE PROMISE 109

I AM HERE 110

AN OPEN HEART 111

A TINY LOVE SONG FOR GOD 112

FOREVER WITH YOU 113

IN YOUR GRACE 114

RISE AND SHINE 115

THE BLESSING 116

JUST ONE 117

THE GIFT 118

HEAVENLY GRACE 119

IT'S ALL A DECISION 120

THE TIME HAS COME 121

MY ILLUMINATION 122

SEARCHING FOR THE ONE 123

6. PRAYER & DEVOTION 124

I WANTED TO BE A NUN 126

TURNING TO GOD 128

I AM YOURS 130

DEVOTED TO YOU 131

THE RETURN 133

THE REMEMBRANCE 134

LISTEN TO LOVE 135

PRAYER TO GOD 136

HUMBLENESS 137

FOREVER WITH HIM 138

BACK TO DIVINITY 139

LONGING FOR YOU 140

TAKE MY HAND 141

A DAILY PRAYER 142

MY BELOVED JESUS 143

THANK YOU 144

EVERY DAY'S MISSION 145

GOD IS 146

A PRAYER TO MY FATHER 147

PART II, QUOTES 148

1. WISDOM 149

2. FREEDOM 171

3. ETERNITY 190

4. COMPLETION 208

AN AFTERTHOUGHT 226

RESOURCES 227

ENDORSEMENTS

With her new book, *All I Am Is Love: Awakening Journey with Divine Poetry and Quotes of Wisdom*, Svava Kristin Love takes us on a beautiful trip to an experience of the Divine. The prose is lovely, the messages profound, and you feel as though an ancient Being is leading you home. This is a great book to calm your mind, open your heart, and be wide open to the realization of Who you really are.
~ Gary R. Renard, best-selling author of *The Disappearance of the Universe* trilogy and *The Lifetimes When Jesus and Buddha Knew Each Other*.

All I Am is Love is filled to overflowing with the riches of the spirit. Svava's pure heart speaks through every page, and will remind you of the immense love in which you are held. I am deeply touched by this immaculate offering, and you will be too. Highly recommended for anyone yearning to remember the miracle you are, and all the gifts of God you deserve!
~ Alan Cohen, best-selling author of *A Course in Miracles Made Easy*, *The Dragon Doesn't Live Here Anymore* and *The Mystical Messiah*.

When you read Svava's new book *All I Am Is Love*, be prepared to be transported. The ideas, the experiences, the quotes, and the poetry will help lift you toward inner happiness and glee, and a feeling of freedom in your heart. The miraculous artistry and eloquence reflect the identity of everlasting Spirit!
~ David Hoffmeister, mystic and author of *This Moment Is Your Miracle*, *Unwind Your Mind Back To God* and *Awakening Through A Course in Miracles*.

All I Am Is Love; A beautiful book infused with authenticity and Love. The gifts of Spirit pour forth from Svava through her story, poetry, quotes and music. Like her music, these wisdom-laden poems transmit the light of awareness directly to the knowing heart, bypassing the confines of the intellect.
~ Nouk Sanchez, best-selling author of *The End of Death* trilogy.

All I Am Is Love is a glimpse into an angel's heart and her journey of remembering Holiness. I am blessed by this Being of Light called Svava. I feel this book expresses all of our yearnings for true connection and love. Jesus says we can learn from others' experiences. Be with it in quiet and receive what is under the words. Thank you Svava Love for sharing your beautiful heart!
~ Suzanne Sullivan, author of *Chip the Monk*, an ACIM-inspired children's book.

Svava is ALL Love and everything that comes through her is from a place of deep devotion to Truth, to God Who Is Love. Her words carry with them a healing frequency of pure Love. Immerse yourself in the beauty, the healing, the peace, the wisdom and the Love found within these pages and breathe.
~ Erin Michelle Galito, mystic and spiritual channel for The Master Jesus.

All I Am Is Love is inspiring and uplifting! Every poem and quote bring you back to your truest Self!
~ Maria Felipe, spiritual teacher and author of *Live Your Happy*.

ABOUT THE AUTHOR

Svava is an Icelandic mystic, singer-songwriter, artist and poet who has devoted her life to awakening and to being a demonstration of love and peace. Svava has had several mystical experiences that began at the age of ten, where she was shown the truth of who we are. In 2016 A Course in Miracles miraculously came into Svava's life. It was a gift from beyond at a very difficult time, and helped her change her mind from fear to love. Svava shares the message that, with forgiveness, true happiness is available right now.

In 2017, without having any training in singing, writing music or playing instruments, Svava began hearing songs and lyrics in mediations and dreams. Svava released her first album, Divine Essence, in 2019, followed by The Light of Truth in 2020, and Grace of God in 2021.

In 2020 Svava began channeling beautiful poetry and quotes. They came as answers to her prayers. This book is a compilation of these prayers and answers.

It only takes an instant to love completely.
~ Svava

DEDICATION

This book is dedicated to all of us on the awakening journey. Every word was given to me as guidance to go from darkness to light. This book is an answer to the prayer of the heart — to know real love; to know Thyself.

I was born the instant I finally loved everything I once feared.
~ Svava

ACKNOWLEDGMENTS

This book would not have been possible if it wasn't for my guide Jesus, the Holy Spirit, the grace of God, Mary Magdalene, Mother Mary, Lady Nada, St. Germain, the Archangels, and my willingness to step into the unknown and listen and follow.

I want to share my deep gratitude for my husband and life companion, David Hoffmeister. You are a beautiful and bright blessing! You have been the most generous trigger in my life, and also a catalyst for helping me step into my purpose. Thank you for your love. Thank you for being a mirror of the truth. Thank you for everything, my beloved. Words cannot describe my deep gratitude.

I want to thank my sweet and loving parents, Sigrun Magnea Joelsdottir and Erling Bjarnason. You have always been there for me and supported me. Thank you for your love.

Deep gratitude to my beautiful sons, Lukas Engilbjartur and Oskar Aðalsteinn. You taught me how to give and how to love unconditionally. Thank you for always reflecting pure innocence back to me. You are a deep blessing and a glorious gift in my life. Thank you. Thank you. Thank you!

Also, many thanks to my friends in the Living Miracles community, and to my friends all over the world who have followed me on social media, listened to my music and my podcast, and supported me in many ways. It is an honor to know you. And at last, countless thanks to my beautiful friends, Olafia Wium and Steven Wiggs for your endless encouragement and your wonderful support. I am forever grateful to you.

Eternal love,
Svava

INTRODUCTION

When I was ten years old, I had a very deep awakening experience. From that moment everything changed for me. I saw behind the veil and experienced the truth of who I am. I do believe that my awakening journey began that day. I didn't understand at that time what was happening to me, but I knew that I had experienced something that wasn't easy to explain. I knew this experience had nothing to do with the world I perceived.

Back then I called my experience, "The Beautiful Nothingness."

It all began when my 7-month-old kitten was hit by a car and passed away. She was, at that time, the love of my life. She slept with me every night, licked my toes in the morning to wake me up, talked back to me with her sweet meow, and was always there for me. I felt like my world had fallen apart when I came home from school and my mom told me that Snotra (an Icelandic name that means Beauty) was dead. I went to my room and cried and cried for hours. The next day when I was supposed to go to school, I never made it inside the building, but sat outside in the schoolyard and cried all day. When the bell rang and the school day was over, I walked back home.

I was almost always alone for some hours after school before my mom would come home from work, so I opened the door to our house with my key and went inside. As I walked inside, I spontaneously looked down the hallway down to the living room, and there I saw my grandmother sitting on the couch with Snotra on her lap and petting her. My grandmother looked up and smiled at me and I smiled back. My grandmother, who I am named after, died when my mom was pregnant with me. I had never seen her before this moment, except in photos. My grandmother telepathically spoke to me and said that Snotra was okay and she would take care of her for me. Then they both disappeared. I went to my room and sat down on my bed, and I began thinking about what is it that dies when we seem to leave this world. I had just seen my grandmother and my kitten. My grandmother had telepathically communicated with me, and I felt that she had spoken to my heart. Since I was very young, I have spoken to God, and I have always felt Jesus very close to me, like my best friend. So in this situation, it was natural for me to turn to God for help. So I asked, "God, can I die?" Suddenly I was somewhere else. I was not in my room, and I was not aware that I had a body. I was just aware that I seemed to be floating weightlessly in an infinite space of beautiful nothingness. I felt so loved and so safe, and it was the most peaceful moment I had ever experienced. I wanted to stay there forever. I felt like I was Home. It felt like a deep recognition within me. It was as if God was all that beautiful, loving, and peaceful space. God was everything, and I was merged with Him—One with it all. I was so happy and peaceful. It all felt complete. It seemed empty but at the same time I knew that everything could spring out of this. It was the core of creation — the Source of all there is.

I have no idea how long I was there. It could have been hours or minutes. Suddenly I was in my room again and I could see my body again. And God had answered my question. I knew from that moment that I could never die. I knew that I was not a body but something wonderful and unexplainable. I knew that my true self will always exist, and I knew that everything that is a part of the made-up world will not last. It comes and goes. I understood that the truth is all there really is and will always be forever and ever. I had an experience of who I am, and this experience has been with me since that day. I believe that it was given to me to begin my journey of awakening. Thank you beloved Snotra for this gift. You are in my heart and with me forever.

I went through many difficult times for many decades after this mystical awakening experience. But the remembrance of the experience often helped me go through the darkness, and it brought me back to the truth over and over.

Often when we have a deep experience of the truth, the darkness will begin to flush up to awareness. And because we have such a deep calling in our hearts to remember who we are, all the blocks to the light have to be brought up to awareness so they can burn away. The journey to awakening from the dream of illusions is not easy. But it IS possible. It is actually inevitable that we remember the love that we are.

All the poems and quotes in this book came to me within two years of my life, probably one of the most difficult periods of my life. It was a time when I felt a very deep loss, devastation and loneliness. I got very sick and was on the edge of giving up on my life. These poems and quotes saved me and pulled me through these years. They popped up in my mind after I had gone through darkness and had insights into what was happening in my mind. They were bringers of clarity, love, joy and peace. Some even brought me into laughter. Thankfully, God often had a way of bringing me into laughter after I had finished crying and feeling sorry for myself. These two years brought me huge strength and certainty of who I truly am.

The poems and quotes were God's answers to questions or topics that I had in mind in the moment. They brought me to an understanding of my thoughts and beliefs and showed me how to forgive. They were my healing journey through those difficult years and an undoing of the false self.

I have often thought about people that have had awakening experiences in devastating situations. I have learned that the most difficult times of my life have been the catalysts for kicking me back Home — back to love; back to the remembrance of who I am. Because in times like that, we have no other way but to turn to God.

The poems and quotes in this book pulled me back into love and peace over and over and taught me that there is a way out of pain and sorrow, when we ask God for help.

If you are reading this book, I know you have been called to wake up to remember who you are. My wish is that this book will be a guide and inspiration for you to follow your heart. Shine your light, Beloved! That is all you need to do. You are so much more than you can imagine. You are the gift of God.

My biggest joy is to be an inspiration to others. It would be my greatest honor if this book could be an inspiration to you.

The art in this book came to me when I was putting this book together.

May God's grace wash away all errors and may the light of truth shine forever in the Holy mind that we share. May there be eternal peace now.

I love you,
Svava

Life is a love affair with God, if we really understood it.
~ Svava

PART 1, POETRY

1. HAPPINESS

A TRUE STORY

The moon danced with the wind tonight.
I saw it with my own eyes.

Then the sun woke up and laughed.
And joined the moon and the wind.

Then the thunder woke up along with the lightning.
They got all fired up and joined the happy dance.
And then the rain appeared and began dancing too.

The earth saw what was going on,
so she began shaking and dancing.
And all this happiness woke up her fire within, along with all the oceans.

And then everything exploded in great joy with dancing northern lights.

I can assure you.
This is all true.
I saw it with my own eyes.

THE HAPPY DREAM

In the presence of Your peace
I feel my own release.
My prayer was to be free.
Now You have answered me.

Everything I thought was real
including the loud voice I could hear,
was all a part of this unreality
— and it was all made up by me.

Now with You by my side
there is nothing to decide.
I am finally free as a bird
and I have no last word.

A soft breeze kisses my cheek.
In the air I hear gentle music.
I look into Your beautiful eyes.
Together now we will arise.

Forever now and here.
I know we are everywhere.
Our love is endless and forever.
One mind and always together.

Thank You for believing in me.
I know this love has set us free.
Everything I now have seen
shows me this is the happy dream.

THIS MOMENT OF JOY!

*Bubbling joy embraces my heart.
A voice says begin from the start.
Nothing needs to ever be the same.
It is possible now to end this game.*

*How can I believe this can be true?
I know my inner child wants to be with You.
But the loud voice tells me to run
and the still voice says it has begun.*

*Child of God there is no turning back.
Nowhere to run, you are right on track.
Trust that I will lead you safe and sound.
My beautiful child, you are finally found.*

*All will be good. Just take his hand.
Do not be afraid. This love will never end.
I did send him to you to comfort your soul
so you both can return completely whole.*

*Trust in Me and follow My voice.
In truth you have just one choice.
To follow your heart that leads you to love
and to open the gate to Heaven above.*

*One light that lights up everything.
One love is all the angels sing.
All is complete and nothing to do.
My beautiful child, I've been waiting for you.*

A RELATIONSHIP JOURNEY

*God brought me
into your vibration.
And He brought you
into my vibration.*

*God had a plan.
A plan to shake up our vibrations.
I guess we had become stuck
— or maybe we were just ready.*

*First it was all calm.
It was as if our vibrations
were getting settled.
— A calmness before the storm.*

*Then the earthquakes began
and the tornados arrived
— wiping out everything
we built to shelter our bodies.*

*Then the volcanos erupted
and the hot lava flowed.
It was hot, so very hot.
And everything turned black.*

*Finally, all became quiet.
Including our minds
— and we woke up.
Everything was gone.
Not a tiny thing had stayed behind.*

We looked at each other
and had no words to say.
Without a word we heard
the beat of our infinite loving vibration.

The Alpha and the Omega.
The beginning and the end.
A black sand full of possibilities.
We looked at each other and smiled.
Do we begin again — or do we just stay here now?

NOTHING HAPPENS BY ACCIDENT

I met you in a big crowd.
And in my shyness,
I tried to hide
behind the people all around.

It was as if time stood still
and sounds disappeared.
It seemed like everything around us
moved in slow motion.

But even though
I tried to be invisible,
I could not prevent
what was meant to be.

As already destined,
our eyes met in a bright blink
— and in deep silence, we merged
into a void of endless light.

Sparkling energies
floating in the air,
like butterflies and fireworks.
— An explosion of love and light.

From this moment
we both knew,
nothing happens by accident.
— Our journey together had begun.

JOYFUL LOVE

One day LOVE said to me,

"Enjoy Me, my beloved. Let your whole being be filled with Me.

Be so filled with Me that I will runneth completely over
and kiss the ground that you stand on."

And just as I felt LOVE under my feet, I burst out laughing.
Because I so easily get very ticklish under my feet.

ETERNAL FRIEND

I saw a glimpse of your light,
shining in the night.
Your true self,
revealed in myself.

Your smile warmed my heart.
You played a perfect part
— pointing me to the now.
Before your feet, I bow.

My beautiful friend,
there will never be an end.
Eternally in God's light,
forever shining bright.

Holy are we,
in love and free.
Shining stars
— divine avatars.

SOFT RELEASE

In the silence of the night
I see the stars shining bright.
My heart rests in Your glory.
I have released my old story.

The past is forgiven.
Only this moment I am living.
In my deep breath, I know
that my life is in a flow.

Nothing to decide.
Nothing to provide.
Everything is given.
In Your love I am driven.

The softness of Your peace
I feel my true release.
I am free to fly with You
and I know Your love is true.

Light as a feather,
we fly in any weather.
Everything is the same
when we share the same name.

You are all of me.
Together we are free.
I finally know who I am.
The world was just a hologram.

THE SOUND OF HEAVEN

In your calm presence
I remember Home.
Safe in your arms
I do not feel alone.

Awake in your glory,
my beautiful friend.
Past our old story,
together we ascend.

High above the oceans.
Far beyond the stars.
We lay aside emotions
as we play our guitars.

The sound of Heaven
sings in our ears.
All is forgiven.
Gone are all our fears.

Forever in this moment,
joined as One heart.
All glory to God.
We will never be apart.

My Holy self, I love you.
My light unites with yours.
Together we call out
to the ones with doubt.

*Our part is to shine bright
and bring everyone back Home.
So all can join in God's light
and no one feels alone.*

DANCING WITH GOD

I saw God dancing
when I told Him my truth.
He looked into my eyes
and He laughed.

I couldn't hold it back
so I burst out laughing too.
What I thought was true
had nothing to do with reality.

God told me that all seriousness
is hiding my bright light.
And that it has to be released
so I again can dance His dance.

The dance of life was waiting for me.
All I needed was to set myself free
from these silly beliefs
— that were never real.

Now I have given it all to Him
to be forever free.
I step into my certainty
so I can dance and laugh into eternity.

A TRUE LOVE SONG

I used to hear all songs
as special love songs.
Then I realized the songs could only be
a deep call that could set me free.

I began to hear myself sing to You.
The lyrics became more true.
Nothing was what I thought was real
and my broken heart began to heal.

Suddenly I heard an angel sing,
"My child go even deeper within.
Reach the corner of your mind
and see what you will find."

I realized the song I sang to You
was a love song for myself.
I fell on my knees and wept
and You kissed me on my forehead.

Could I be the love I always longed for?
Was I all this time searching for myself?
Oh my love, I am this love!
One with You in the Heavens above.

BEGIN ANEW

When thoughts spin around,
focus on the sound.
The quiet wave
that God gave.

His gifts to you
point you to what is true.
That you are His child,
running in the wild.

Stop playing the game
— it is all the same.
No peace can be found
where you feel bound.

Give Him your troubles
to put inside bubbles.
Send them away
and begin a new day.

GRATITUDE

I have accepted my savior.
My savior is you.
I judged your behavior
and I missed out on the truth.

You showed me my mind,
all obstacles to God's light.
Oh I was so blind.
I had denied His sight.

You showed me how to look.
It was a roller coaster ride.
I often felt hanging on a hook.
Or thrown to the side.

It was all my own loop.
A meaningless story.
I needed to be scooped
— up to God's glory.

I tried to refuse His love,
but I fell deeper into pain.
I longed to see above it all
and I almost went insane.

God called onto me.
Guided me to be free.
Told me the story wasn't me
and showed me how to truly see.

So you, my savior,
I thank you with all my heart.
You did me a favor.
We will never be apart.

Beyond the world of form.
Shining in God's light.
Bodies are transformed.
All is love and all is bright.

BORN TO FLY

You were born to fly
but you cannot see your wings.

You were born to be the best version of yourself
but you have bound your wings with a rope
so they cannot move — not even an inch.

You were born to fly above this world
and lead the way for the ones that have forgotten their wings as well.

You must untie the rope that is binding your wings
so you can spread your wings and show everyone how to fly.

The rope might be filled with shame, judgments and unworthiness.
But be not disheartened my beloved,
I am here with you.

And when you fly, everyone will fly.

A GLORIOUS MELT

I have lost myself in this glorious instant.
I have lost myself in love.
I have lost all thoughts of past and future
and melted with You now.

Endless peace abides in me
and my heart is wide open.
Completely out of time and space,
I find myself in joy.
Laughing at what never was,
I sing Your Heavenly song.

All my brothers and sisters I invite to join with me
so we all can sing and laugh and dance
— and then melt with eternity.

THE BREATH OF MY SOUL

My soul is the breath of the universe.
It brings life into everything I see.
For without the breath of my soul
nothing would seem to exist.

In my breath I create all beings.
I create everything I see.
With a gentle breath, I see clearly
all the beauty and the truth surrounding me.

If I forget the purpose of the universe
and lose awareness of my breath,
I become a lost soul in endless space
— blind, confused and unable to create.

So with a simple and gentle awareness
of a soft and peaceful breath,
I beam into the depths of the universe
and create as my true self.

YOU SPEAK TO ME IN SYMBOLS

Symbols, Oh my God.
You show me so many symbols — and signs.
The symbols show me You are here.
Signs and symbols that guide me everywhere.

It seems so simple, my God.
It seems I need to do nothing on my own.
Just simply follow Your symbols and signs
— so I can see far beyond all timelines.

You speak to me, God, without ceasing.
In every step I take.
Every day a penny shows up on the ground
and You say,
"My love, with Me, your life is unbound."

I wake up every morning
serenaded by singing birds.
Their divine songs remind me of You
and tell me that each moment is new.

After the rain I breathe the fresh air.
It fills my lungs with Your soft grace.
I smell all the beautiful flowers
and merge with their Heavenly powers.

Oh my God, I can see You are never absent.
You are everywhere I look, and in every sound, I hear.
You whisper to me that I am One with You.
So, oh God, I must be everywhere too.

And then You say,
"My love, this is all for you."

IF GOD WOULD ASK

If God would ask me,
"Svava, which experiences in your life have brought you to Me?"

I would say,
"All of them God. Especially the ones that broke my heart."

2. MYSTICAL LIFE

A CUP OF WONDER

I look at my coffee cup
and I wonder

— would it be there
if I didn't look at it?

Or does it appear
because I'm looking at it?

With a humble heart,
I tune deeper within.

And I realize,

no matter
how many thinkable tricks
I try to do,
to understand if the cup is there
when I'm not looking.
I will never really know.

Because, when I'm not looking at the cup,
it's seemingly gone.
And it seems to appear
when I look again.

So maybe everything transforms into images
when I give it attention.
Maybe I'm making everything up!!!

Hmmmmm...

Can I rest in the not knowing?

This question expands my mind.
And I realize on a much deeper level, the only choice there always is
— this moment of peace.

Ahhhhhhhhhh!
So simple and so wonderful.

My purpose and my only function.

Peace.
Simply just peace.

THE ANGEL

I met an angel today
— a very tall and beautiful angel.

His wings were majestic, and his eyes glowed like the stars in the sky.
The angel told me that anything I can imagine can happen.

He told me that I can dance down the river,
jump between the clouds,
fly through the forest
and see through the eyes of an eagle.

The angel told me, there are no limits to my imagination
and to what I can do.

He also told me, that all these things I can imagine
are not my heart's true desire.
For even though I could do and have anything I can imagine,
none of these imaginings could ever fulfill my heart's true desire.

Then the angel bowed down and whispered in my ear,
"What is your heart's true desire?"

I closed my eyes, took a deep breath, and paused for a moment
before I said,
"To softly rest in the vastness of the power before any imaginings."
And the angel gently responded with a smile on his beautiful face,
"That would be resting in your true self."

FALLING FILTERS

What you believe,
will seem real
to you.
What your brother believes,
will seem real
to him.

Even though you try to share
what you see
with your brother,
he won't see
what you see
— as he only sees
through a filter
of his own beliefs.

And when he tries to share
with you
what he sees,
you won't see
what he sees

— as it will be
filtered
through your
own beliefs.
But!!!
Deep within you both
is the infinite.

Call it love, call it light
— or call it anything you want.
Words cannot describe it.

Only the indescribable can truly be shared.
— And only in silence.
For if you try to put words to it,
it will go through filters
and not be experienced for what it is.

So close your eyes and tune in.
Stay with what is.
Let the filter fall away.
Let your experience of the truth be what you extend.
And let the truth be how you show up in the world.

LIQUID LOVE

I drank from the glass
of Your liquid love.

The love that floods
all over this world.

I drank of this powerful substance,
which everything is made of.

I thought I drank it all up,
but the glass kept on filling up
— simply by itself.

It was as if it was endless.

There was always more
where it came from.

So without any effort,
to this day,

I simply keep on drinking
of the glass of liquid love.

A HEAVENLY TUNE

In the stillness of my heart,
I rest in Your warmth.
Nothing but my thoughts
can bring us apart.

In the quiet of my mind,
I hear Your soft voice
whisper to my soul,
"Your thoughts are your choice."

When only Your love
I choose to bring
— into my Holy mind,
I hear angels sing.

A choir of peace.
A glorious sound.
A gentle release
lifts me from the ground.

With angel wings,
I feel only You.
My heart filled with love,
I sing Your heavenly tune.

RETURNING TO PEACE

Trust in Me and relax.
Let Me lift you up on the eagle's back.

Listen to the sound of the majestic wings.
Hear the eternal song of Heaven sing.

It is calling you to open your heart of love.
To bring you to the Heavens above.

Close your eyes and look at Me.
Feel My love that sets you free.

Breathe the love, take it in.
This changeless love has always been.

You are it, and it is you.
An innocent heart knows this is true.

Return to the truth, return to Me.
And let My love set you free.

THE DIVINE BEING

From my thoughts
you appeared.

I saw you as a divine being.
Beaming with glorious light.

Your smile lit up the whole universe.
And your eyes were bright like a beautiful star.

All around you I saw the most amazing colors.
Colors so bright that I cannot describe them in words.

I thought of you as the most magnificent thing I've ever seen.
Nothing can be compared with this beauty.

And then I thought,
if I can think these thoughts
and feel all this beauty within me,
then you must be in me
and I must be in you.

So we must be this One divine being,
shining in the most glorious light
— and beaming out colors
that cannot be described in words
We must be this One magnificence.

CERTAINTY

Suddenly the certainty was here,
all around me and within me.
It had merged with me completely
— like a wave of infinite power!

It was as it had sneaked upon me,
touched me on my head
and kissed me on my cheeks
— without me even noticing.

For so long I had been longing
to know certainty — to truly know!
So that I could peacefully just be.

I had not understood
the real power of certainty.
Not until I had really understood
who I truly am.

With the love for myself
washing over me,
came the love for everyone
— and the realization
there was only One to love.

Then suddenly the certainty was here,
like a wave of an unexplainable grace
that filled my whole being
with vast and infinite love.

*Certainty,
completely absent of doubt!
An unwavering knowledge
of who I am
— that I simply just am
love.*

A TRUE REFLECTION

I look at the sky, and I see You.
I look at the sun, and I see You.
I look at the ocean, and I see You.
I look at the trees, and I see You.
I look at a flying eagle, and I see You.
I look at a friend, and I see You.
I look at my finger pointing to the sun, and I see You.

Everywhere I look, I see You.
You must be in my eyes because I see only You.
You must be in my mind because I think like You.
You must be in all of me because I feel You.
My heart is filled with love for You.
Within my whole being, I know You.
You are everywhere, and so must I be too.
I am here only to remember what is true.
That I was always One with You.

Thank You.

CLUELESSNESS

I did not understand.
Maybe I still do not know.
All I could feel was a broken heart
and loss of my breath.
Something seemed to die
— but maybe it was all good.
I am still not sure if it was for my best.
I am not even sure where I am,
what I am doing;
or where I am going — if anywhere.

I follow a spark and just keep on sharing my light.
Maybe I am on the right track now;
maybe I am not.
Maybe I fell again and do not know it yet.
I do not know anything.
All I have is faith.
I am trying to understand how it all works.

Sometimes I feel tricked
and sometimes I feel like a fool.
And then I rise up again
with a grateful heart.
The love in my heart is always there.
It seems like it will not go away
no matter what.
It feels changeless even when I seem to be down.

Maybe that is all I need to know
— the changeless love beyond it all.

Maybe I am on the right track after all.
Sometimes I do feel that I am.
I pray that everything will be okay.
I pray that I will find myself in it all.
I pray that I will see that everything
that happened was because I am loved.
I want to know just that.
That I am loved.

That is all.

CONSISTENCY

The sky seems cloudy and gray
and the streets are filled with puddles.
But my Holy mind is here to stay
and the light in me never goes away.

No matter the form I see,
joy and peace remain within me.
I can dance in the rain and sing to the sky.
Nothing can stop me — I take off and fly.

When my mind is filled with You,
I cannot see but what is true.
Heart filled with love and eyes full of light.
Show me the reflection of true sight.

My vision shows me eternal peace.
This is my point of complete release.
A changeless being, ready to fly.
It is time to let it all pass by.

Free am I, forever in You.
Everything begins anew.
In a free fall I enter the abyss
and in ecstasy, I embrace Your infinite bliss.

THE MYSTICAL PLACE

In the presence of You
I smile and soar.
All I see now is brand new.
This is everything I longed for.

My heart is overflowing
with Your glorious grace.
My pure light is glowing
in this mystical place.

My vision is bright and clear.
I have awoken to Your bliss.
All my ears clearly can hear
is Your soft and loving kiss.

Stillness embraces all of my being.
I'm gently floating in empty space.
Nothing to hold on to — it is so freeing.
Now Your heavenly light is my face.

Forever as One, we happily shine.
I look at You and I see the beautiful me.
Everything is complete and divine.
With You, my love, I am eternally free.

A BEAUTIFUL DREAM

I dreamt that I was a woman
— a beautiful one that loved to love.

A woman that longed for a kind man, and a house,
and a car, and also a cute cat.
A cozy house with a fireplace, an ocean view
and a sweet smell of freshly baked bread.

A happy woman with a simple life.
A kind woman that loved it all.

It was a beautiful dream of pure happiness.
A dream that I will keep in my heart.

Thank You, God.

MY LIFE

I am determined to live so fully,
so that when I lay aside my body
I can take my last breath
with a big smile on my face
and say,
"Wow, that was amazing."
And my last thought would be,

"Thank You, God."

UNCONDITIONAL LOVE

I have met you in countless lifetimes.
I have loved you in many different forms.
I even loved you when you seemed to hate me,
and I have held you in my arms when you tried to push me away.

I have stroked your hair when you felt pain.
I have kissed your tears when you felt sorrow.
I have loved you through everything
and through countless lifetimes.

I have loved you in many different places
— on earth and far beyond through the endless space.
And even though your form has changed
over and over and over, this deep love has always remained.

You are the breath that I take,
and the wind beneath my wings.
You are the light that I see and the melody I hear.
You are the bubbling joy in my belly
and the warmth that embraces my heart.

You are the light that lifts me up to the glorious vastness of infinity.
Nothing you do can ever change my love for you
— because this love is changeless and eternal.

All I can do is love because love is who I am.
And all I perceive is love because love is who you are.
There is nothing but love.

YOU ARE WHAT I AM

In my emptiness, I saw You,
absent of everything except Your love.
You are my food, and You are my drink.
You are my voice, and You are my sight.

My heart burns for You
and Your love awakens my passion.

All that I extend is You.
The light that I have released is You.
It reflects like stars in the ocean
and dances softly on the horizon.

Nothing of this world can contain
Your infinite love and Your eternal light.

Behind the veil of illusions, the vastness of You appears.
And what I thought I was now vanishes into nothingness.

I merge with Your magnificence
and return to my true being.
Love is my whole existence.
In Your arms I am.
I am a Spirit of love and One with You.

WHO AM I?

I asked God,
"Who am I?"
And He answered,
"Svava, who do you think you are?"

I paused and replied,
"God, I can't think who I am."
And God responded,
"Exactly Svava, you are beyond thinking."

LOVE AND BLESSINGS

May your heart be filled with love.
May your eyes be filled with light.
May your nose be filled with the smell of roses,
and may your ears hear the hymns of Heaven.

Eternal love and blessings, beloved One.

3. TRANSFORMATION

THANKFULNESS

Thankfulness.
Oh yes, thankfulness!
So simple and yet so powerful.
It can beam you out
of any distorted thought,
you mistakenly might have picked up.

Oh yes, it is that simple!
Just a shift into thankfulness,
and immediately, you are lifted up
into the eternal vastness
of God's shining glory.

— Even though
it sometimes seems
like everything
is crashing,

then oh yes, thankfulness
is always the magical key.
It can open your heart in an instant
and fill it up with love.

So yes,
thankfulness!

Always!

THE CHOICE

*Oh, Holy One,
the time has come.
To set yourself loose
— it is time to choose.*

*The seeming choices
are between two voices.
But only one is true
and that one is You.*

*So, how to know?
How to be in the flow?
And hear only the true voice
and not the loud noise.*

*The truth feels like ahhhhhh
and not like blah blah blah.
So how you feel
will tell you which voice is real.*

*So in this beautiful instant
where there is no distance,
is your freedom and release
from the voice of disease.*

*Your true choice is peace
in this moment of release.
When you see what is real
you will know how to heal.*

*Your purpose is to love,
to stay in His presence high above.
And to bathe in His divine glory
— where everything is extraordinary.*

STILLNESS

On a still day,
I know the way.
I hear Your voice
when there is no noise.

When my thoughts do block,
I get confused and stuck.
So I look up and pray,
You will take these thoughts away.

I close my eyes and make a choice,
to listen only to Your still voice.
You are my life and my love.
In Your presence, I rest above.

ASCENSION

Sacred union
in the arms of love.
I have longed for this reunion
with You above.

My heart feels free.
My light shines bright.
Finally, I can be me
— a pure shining light.

I simply extend
what You gave to me.
I am ready to ascend
and set myself free.

Lifted up by Your glory.
Weightless and safe.
I renounce the old story.
You whisper that I am brave.

I am ready to merge,
eternally with You!
To leave the earth
and to know what is true.

TRUST

The path is all set.
You need but follow.
A dive into the depth
to let go of all sorrow.

Trust is required
— a complete let go.
True love desired
and a merge with the flow.

With heart wide open,
bright light flows within.
No words are spoken
— now undoing can begin.

Dark clouds move through.
Let them all pass by.
It is an illusion of you.
It was all just a lie.

Merge with the light.
Take it all in.
Let your truth shine bright
— now your life can begin.

All you are is pure light.
All you share is true love.
Eternally so bright
— in God's glory above.

TRANSFORMATION

What I perceive
must be healed,
as it cannot be
that this is real.

Fragments of insanity
call for liberty.
I pray for redemption
— for a real perception.

Spirit, I call upon You.
Show me a world that is true.
A clear vision of peace
— resting on a soft breeze.

You whisper,
"Come with me. Peace will set you free."
I feel Your kiss on my cheek
and we walk into the mystique.

You show me clarity
— a mind that is free.
A child of wonder
that was hidden down under.

Below distorted sight
is the being of light.
Free from all lies
— a child of paradise.

THE KIND VOICE

A spark of light
brightens up the night.
A gentle voice
whispers my choice,

"Follow me
and set yourself free.
Take a leap
or stay asleep."

I hear Your voice.
I know my choice.
Tempted though, to stay
focused, on my own way.

I will not lie,
I often do cry
— when I see the truth
with Your eyes.

With You I see it all.
With You there was no fall.
Oh God, now I can see
I was always free.

STARING AT THE OCEAN

I stare at the big ocean.
It moves in slow motion.
Here time seems nonexistent
and I feel completely consistent.

The wild wind clears my mind.
This view is one of a kind.
High waves dancing and free,
they remind me of the power in me.

The rain gently kisses my face.
This power, this love, and this grace.
All meet in this mystical empty space,
where creation takes place.

It all begins where it all ends.
One point that ascends.
All of this is nothing and everything
— just wait and see what it will bring.

Get ready for the big eruption.
It will take you into a flotation,
where new fire will begin to burn
and get you ready for your return.

AWAKENING

In my sleep I dreamt of fear,
fear that took me nowhere.
Then I saw it was all unreal
and my heart began to heal.

Suddenly my eyes could see
all around me was gentle glee.
Darkness changed into light,
and I saw with true sight.

I saw You in everything.
I saw what Your love could bring.
I knew that all I was was light.
Eternally shining bright.

KNOWING YOU

Today I was washed with Your grace.
It kissed me on my forehead and
pulled me into a wave of love.
My dancing heart jumped with joy
and my soul burst out laughing.

Oh, my God
I recognized You.
All of You was all of me
and all of me was You
— as One dancing in the light of truth.

This wave of love still lives in me.
This joy still plays around my heart.
Now, tomorrow, always, and forever
will this magnificent light remain.
All that is required is simply to remember.

THE ULTIMATE QUESTION

*If you asked me,
"How can I find God?"*

*I would say,
"There is nothing but God. Open your eyes, my friend,
and you will see God."*

*Then you might say,
"There must be something wrong with my eyes,
because I cannot see God."*

*And my answer would be,
"Then you must wash away that which is blocking your sight.
Because God is in everything
— including you."*

WHY I CAME

I came here to share,
to share my love and compassion.

I came here to be kind,
and to hold your hand when needed.

I also came to kiss your cheeks
— when they call for it.

And if I forget my mission
please bear with me.

I'm committed to do my best
to remember why I came here.

And I know in my heart
that you came here for this too.

So, let's see the beauty within us.
Let's take each other's hands
and run happily through the forest,
or dance by the ocean

— knowing that we are in this together.

And simply just walking each other Home.

YOUR BEAUTY

The beauty I see in you
is a reflection of the truth.

Your bright shining colors
shine on my soul
and awaken me from an illusionary dream.

These colors embrace my loving heart
and lift me up into the light of truth,

where we sing and dance in God's glory
as the happy children He created us to be.

Thank you, my beloved friend.
Thank you for being here with me.
Thank you for walking with me hand in hand.
And thank you for never leaving me.

For only together will we enter into eternity
— the infinite light that is our Home.

When we finally see that we are the same,
all fear will vanish and will be forgotten forever
— and the dream will be over.

All that remains when we awaken
is eternal love that shines so bright.
A loving light so magnificent
that no words can describe it.

*One bright, loving light
that merges with eternity
— and finally returns to God.*

BELOVED ONE

I know you have realized
that you didn't come here
to be sad and frustrated.

You must know by now
that there is
a divine plan beyond it all.

So often have you questioned,
"Why am I here
and what is really going on?"

It all has seemed cryptic
at times
— and often very confusing.

But I know that you have not
been able to completely ignore
the symbols I have given you.

I speak to you
everywhere you look
and in every sound, you hear.

Simply watch and listen
in silence
— and without a word.

Give! My beloved, just give!
And let your divine love
feed the thirsty on earth.

Your part is that simple
and so very easy.
Just be You.
Be love.

YOUR PURPOSE

Your presence is a gift of love.
Your breath is a breeze of softness.
Your eyes are a mirror of light.
Your smile is an invitation to joy.
Your heart is a beat of life.
Your voice is a song of Heaven.
Your hands are the bringers of kindness.
And your feet are gently leading you Home.

ARISE SOUL, ARISE!

Arise soul, arise!
Arise from the ashes
and into the light.

Arise from the dusty
and thirsty ground,
and merge with the light of love.

Let the loving light that shines forever
hold you tight and lift you up.
Let it welcome you
into the depth of your own being.

Just let yourself fall!
Fall deeply into this loving light
— this loving light that lives within you.

Arise soul, arise!
Arise from the ashes
and return to yourself.

NOW

My beloved child of light,
I have come to wake you up from the illusion of time.
I have come to bring you back into the awareness of eternity.
There is no time, and there never was.
There is only now
— and there is no need to linger in unreality anymore.

Nothing is holding you back from realizing your true nature now
except a belief in something unreal
— and this belief is obscuring your true identity in Me.

You have mistakenly believed in linear time
instead of the infinite now.
I created you in my image, therefore, nothing not of Me is true.
You are One with Me eternally,
and no belief can ever change this fact.

Rejoice with Me in our Oneness now.
Come and dance with Me into eternity.
I love you now.

WHAT IS REAL?

"What is real?" I asked.
And He answered, "You are."

I smiled and said, "Then, what am I?"

And He responded,
"In the absence of what will decay, you are."

Then I replied,
"Well, then I must be something
that cannot be measured or touched."

"Precisely," He responded.

Then everything was still.

BEYOND THE BODY

The body plays no part in eternity.
The body plays no part in peace.
The body plays no part in the light.
And the body plays no part in love.
Eternity, peace, light, and love are One.
Oneness beyond the body is all there is.

LET GOD SHOW YOU THE WAY

Let your eyes see the beauty of yourself.
Let your ears hear the sound of silence.
Let your lips taste the softness of the air.
Let the breeze of life kiss your cheeks.
Let your feet walk on clear water.
Let your hair dance in the sun.
Let your innocence embrace night and day.
Let God show you the way.

4. LOVE & LIGHT

A HOLY MOMENT

I met a stranger at a cafe today
and I looked him in the eye.

"I think I know you," he said.
I smiled and replied,
"Yes, of course, you know me."

— Because,
how could we not know each other,
when we are the same?

Then I invited him to join me for a cup of coffee
— like we were old friends that just happened to meet again.

Happily he accepted,
with a beautiful bright glow all around him.

And from that moment there was no doubt,
we had always been friends.

DANCE WITH THE STARS

Your melody of peace
sings softly of my release.
Brings me to the light
and wipes out the night.

This Heavenly tune
lifts me to the moon,
where I dance with the stars
— all the way to Mars.

Happy and in love
in the Heavens above.
With You by my side
and my heart open wide.

I softly sing Your song,
in Your arms where I belong.
You gently touch my hair.
With You, I am everywhere.

THE SONG OF THE LIGHT

Close your eyes
and listen to the song of the light.

Its vibration sings to the beat of your heart
and makes it glow like a thousand stars.

All worries and doubts vanish in the song of the light,
and your whole being serenades in its loving sounds.

If you surrender deeper and deeper
and let the song take you along;
you will feel it lift you higher and higher
— far away from all worldly sounds.

The song of the light has no ending
— nor did it have a beginning.
It sings forever its glorious melody.

Like you this song always was and always will be.
The song of the light is you!

UNDEFINED ONENESS

Under the sky,
both of us fly.
Holy as One,
next to the sun.

Stars radiate deep peace,
guide us to our release.
Expansion of our light,
and eyes shining bright.

Never lost to you,
committed to what is true.
Changeless love,
in God's arms above.

In deep gratitude,
everyone I include.
One heart and One mind,
that cannot be defined.

HOW TO KNOW TRUE LOVE

To understand love,
you need to sit on the back of an eagle
— not knowing where you are going.

When a wind comes, you have to hold on
and let go of all your fearful thoughts about falling off.

When a storm comes,
you have to be even more vigilant of your thoughts,
and hold on even tighter.
You have to trust that the eagle knows the direction.

One sunny day you will stop being afraid of falling off.
You will sing a song to the Heavens and rejoice.

When your mind becomes completely still,
the eagle will softly lay you down on a flowerbed
and kiss your forehead.

Only when the mind is completely free from fear,
true love can be known.

UNION

I feel your light
in the quiet rest.
In your beautiful eyes,
I feel so blessed.

My heart beats
in your still presence.
I take a deep breath
and feel our essence.

Our souls merge.
Two hearts as One.
Surrendered to Holiness,
where we belong.

I am you now.
You are me too.
Separation is gone,
forever as new.

This Holy instant
is all that is true.
A glorious gratitude
— and I love you.

HOLY MOTHER

Oh, Holy Mother of all.
In Your warm arms, I must fall.
Unwrap me from my clouds
and wash away my doubts.

In Your bright shining light,
my eyes are gifted with true sight.
I see myself in Your eyes.
There will be no more goodbyes.

I invite You here to stay,
to be with me when I pray.
So, I never will forget
the beautiful day we met.

CALLING YOU

My heart called Your name.
Immediately You came.
Your voice calmed my mind
when my sight seemed blind.

You whispered in my ear,
"Let go of the fear.
I am here by your side.
Come into the light."

You took my hand.
We flew to the promised land.
My mind was free
and my heart filled with glee.

I danced in Your glory.
Free from all worry.
In Your arms forever.
Eternally together.

ONE HEART

In the stillness of the deep ocean,
I meet my true devotion.
A deep call in my heart, I hear
and Your love becomes clear.

I give all of me to You
to let Your love shine through.
All that I give I become,
and with You I am One.

My heart's true desire
is to bring love higher.
For all to see their divinity
and to know eternity.

I know Your love is real.
I have seen Your love can heal.
For all fear in me is gone
and I can fly like a swan.

Free as a bird on a clear day,
with no words left to say.
Nothing to weigh me down.
I am far away from the ground.

Always and forever.
I know we are together.
One love and One heart.
And never apart.

THE LIGHT HAS COME

The light has come
to lighten up my mind.
Everything is done,
and nothing left to find.

Love has awoken
in my heart of gold.
No words are spoken,
and nothing to behold.

In His grace I softly rest
and let everything go.
In His arms I feel blessed
and my heart starts to glow.

Forever at Home.
Eternally in His love.
I was never alone.
Blessed in the Heavens above.

INFINITE BLISS

Your Holiness is all I see.
In that purity I set myself free.
Holding Your hand into eternity.
In Your grace, I will always be.

The waves of light embrace my soul.
They wash my mind and make me whole.
Your presence is all I long for.
In Your arms, I softly soar.

Taken by the glory of Your love.
I rest in the Heavens above.
All is well and always will be.
With You, I can truly see.

All there is and always will be
is this changeless eternal glee.
All that happened was I forgot the key.
The key to my heart that has set me free.

Now forever in Your glorious light.
An infinite bliss shining bright.
I was always One with You.
Now I feel my soul born anew.

My heart is open, the door is gone.
I know I am forever the Holy One.
I feel Your love, I know who I am.
The world I saw was just a hologram.

TRUE LONGING

In your eyes I see you.
I see you long for what is true,
to break through the ice
and to finally rise.

I long to hold your hand
and bring you to the promised land,
where we become One
and merge with Heaven's song.

My heart calls out to you.
God says He needs two,
to turn all the rocks
and let go of the blocks.

All that is required
is a deep desire,
to know only love
in Heaven above.

Will you come with me?
— So we can set ourselves free.
I am here with you now.
Let God show us how.

All that I long for
is for us to soar,
in the grace of His peace
— for our complete release.

*Trust me and come
to a place where we belong.
Let us go together
and be as One forever.*

ENTERING THE LIGHT

Deep inside of me
where my soul abides.
My love for you is free
and my light is your light.

I accept you as you are
because I accept the truth of me.
You are never very far;
in my mind, it is you I see.

In this glorious moment
joining in God's love.
We accept the Atonement
and dance in the Heavens above.

So to you, my friend, I bow
and my lips kiss your feet.
Together we found the how
and only in God's love we meet.

Free as flying eagles,
we fly through the night.
Together as equals,
we enter the light.

So thank you, my friend
with all my grateful heart.
You are a Godsend.
Now our One life can start!

LOVE AND FEAR

Love does not see fear
because love knows only love.

When fear sees love
it runs away and hides.

Although deep inside
fear wants to merge with love.

But as it is fear, its role is to be afraid.

Afraid of fading
into nothingness

— and becoming love that does not see fear.

Would you merge with love
and let go of everything else?

If you are brave enough to do so
you will realize,
that love was always all you were
and fear was just a thought.

AND SO IT IS

This day we dedicate to love, peace and joy!

May this day be so filled with miracles
that all we are aware of is the truth of who we are.
Everything untrue will fall away like dead leaves on a tree.

May our hearts and minds be so filled
with love and compassion
for everyone and everything — including ourselves,

that we beam out of the dream world of fear
and merge with the happy dream of non-judgments.

May the light of truth shine through us
and bring the truth into every heart and mind we meet
— or think of today.

May we be lifted into the arms of true love today
and rest in the glory of God — in eternity.

LOST IN LOVE

I lost myself in love.
Then I realized that I was love.
Then I knew that I was never lost
and I realized that I was found.

LOVE IS

Love is giving
Love is selfless
Love is courageous
Love is formless
Love is limitless
Love is universal
Love is unconditional
Love is abundance
Love is inclusive
Love is peaceful
Love is happiness
Love is joyful
Love is freedom
Love is generous
Love is kindness
Love is commitment
Love is respectfulness
Love is communication
Love is patience
Love is creation
Love is certainty
Love is changeless
Love is infinite
Love is unity
Love is now
Love is oneness
Love is salvation
Love is you
Love is God
Love is
Love

I SEE YOU

All my life I have been looking for You.
And now I see You.
My eyes rest in Your beauty
and my soul lays humble before Your light.
In You I know who I am.
A divine being of light so pure
and glowing in eternal glory.
A light embraced in a magnificent stillness
and praised forever in love's divine grace.
Humble, I kneel before Your feet;
You, glorious holiness, sent from the Heavens
to show me who I am.
You have breathed real life in me.
A love so magnificent
that no human form can ever understand it.
Before Your glorious light I finally see who I am.
I am You.

5. GRACE

UNEXPLAINABLE PERFECTION

Sometimes I call You God.
Sometimes I call You Spirit.
Other times I just call You What Is.
And sometimes I call You Source
— or Creator of everything.

I could also call You Universe.
Or I could call You Almighty
— or simply just Unconditional Love.
But truly it does not really matter.

You are the core foundation of all there Is.
You are the changeless truth
that breathes life into everything.
All there Is comes from You.

Everything Is You!

There cannot be any other explanation.
I must be like You,
and all that I create must be like You too.

Nothing cannot be but One with You.
Then — oh yes, everything must be perfect!
It is impossible that it could be otherwise.

So, I could call myself all these beautiful words
that I use for You.

I could even come up with many more.

I could call myself divine, a pure light
or a Heavenly being.

But the most important is to know
— to truly know that there is no difference
between You and me or anyone else.

Nothing can be but the same.

Just One unexplainable perfection!

THE PROMISE

God promised me
that I would return to Him at last.

So even though I sometimes seem lost,
I always remember His promise.

Because I know in my heart
that His words are forever true.

So, one beautiful day
God will call me back Home.

It will be the day when I have completed
all my lessons.

And meanwhile, I enjoy His daily gifts to me
by happily giving them away.

I AM HERE

Once I asked God,

"How can I remember You each moment of my life?"

And His answer to me was,

"How could you ever forget me my child,
when I am all you see, all you hear,
all you smell, all you taste, and all you touch?"

And then He continued,

"It is impossible that I can ever be absent from you, my beloved.
So let Me remind you, in each moment of your life, I am here.
This will help you remember."

♡

AN OPEN HEART

My heart is open like a lotus flower.
Colors of light flow through it like a river.
With my arms wide open, I let it all shiver
and an ecstatic energy lifts me up.

Passion opens my glorious channels.
Surrendering to this indescribable bliss.
I let myself fall deep into the abyss
where an explosion of fire awakens within.

The experience brings up bright sparkles.
An energy that gives birth to creation.
Passion is my key to salvation.
It wakes up all that has been hidden inside.

There is no time to waste on silly illusions.
Get ready for a joyful ride.
Now is the time to fully decide.
Would you take my hand
and join me in the ecstasy of life?

A TINY LOVE SONG FOR GOD

Your grace illuminates me.
In Your presence, my heart is free.
With Your patience and trust in me,
I have the courage to set myself free.

FOREVER WITH YOU

My heart aches for You.
Oh God, help me through
this dark devastation,
into Your soft salvation.

All I long to do
is forever to be with You.
Rest in Your sweet grace,
far away from this worldly maze.

Down by Your feet,
I hear my heartbeat.
Calling out to be
with You and forever free.

You touch my head.
You whisper, "Do not be sad.
My child you are One with me
and you were always free."

Awake in Your glory.
Free from the illusionary story.
Forever here with You
and merged with what is true.

IN YOUR GRACE

When I see the light
I hold on tight,
to the grace that I feel
— for only that is real.

I open my heart
so I will never depart
from the truth that I feel.
Heaven is real.

I rest in Your grace,
in a Holy place.
My mind is free.
Now my eyes can see.

All is true love
in the Heavens above.
Nothing else is true
and my heart belongs to You.

With You, I know.
In Your presence, I glow
like a star in the sky.
God, I am ready to fly.

RISE AND SHINE

Rise, my beloved!
Rise with the sun when it rises in the morning.

Shine, my beloved!
Shine like the sun shines through the day.

— And don't get fooled by clouds, my beloved.
For nothing can stop the sun from shining above the clouds.

Rest, my beloved!
Rest with the sun in its evening setting.

Be still, my beloved!
Be still and listen to your beautiful heart.

How wonderful and peaceful it is
to rest with a heart full of light.

— For how could your heart not be overflowing with light
after a whole day of shining!

♡

THE BLESSING

In the stillness of love,
divinity embraces me.
In Your presence above,
I float in eternity.

Beyond what I see
abides Your Heavenly light.
It shines bright on me
and erases the night.

All I perceive now
is a beautiful paradise.
To You, my Lord, I bow
— and in the light, I rise.

No words left to say
in Your divine rest.
I am here to stay
— eternally blessed.

JUST ONE

I am you.
You are me.
We are One
in eternity.

THE GIFT

My gift is my love.
It is all that I have
so it is all that I can give.

In the presence of love
I am completely speechless.
This divine love has no words.

So in silence, I just am.
Love is what I am.
There is nothing else.

Just a still and loving presence.
That is all.
And everything.

HEAVENLY GRACE

Joined in Holy purpose
united in soft grace,
where the divine smell of roses
pulls us out of the maze.

Where tears used to fall
now the flowers happily grow.
They've taken all our sorrows
so love can freely flow.

A deep look into beautiful eyes
and a gentle kiss on a warm cheek.
A heavenly smell of the divine
brings us into the mystique.

Finally, I can show you what I see.
A true sight of pure divinity.
This glorious realm absent of words
— a mystical place of infinity.

Where creation has its beginning,
we stand in empty space.
With divine love all around us,
we rest forever in Heavenly grace.

IT'S ALL A DECISION

Kindness is a decision.
Happiness is a decision.
Joy is a decision.
Love is a decision.
Peace is a decision.
Gratitude is a decision.
Freedom is a decision.
Salvation is a decision.
Light is a decision.
Truth is a decision.
Heaven is a decision.
God is a decision.

It's all a decision!

THE TIME HAS COME

My beloved One,
the time has come.
To let God decide
and go into the light.

Nothing here
takes you anywhere.
Only with Me
can you set yourself free.

Open your mind.
In your heart, you will find
the truth you came here for.
It's time to completely soar.

Rest in God's grace
in this Holy place.
Where all is One
and the light has come.

It is all complete now.
To you, my love, I bow.
Eternally with you.
Now all becomes new.
Thank you for your devotion.

MY ILLUMINATION

My life is an instant, illuminated by light.
My heart is wide open, glowing bright.
My eyes rest in Your infinite grace
— and Your kindness kisses my beautiful face.

SEARCHING FOR THE ONE

I have been searching for You all my life.
The One that brings joy in my heart.
The One that lights up my eyes.
The One that has all the answers to my questions.
The One that loves me unconditionally and to eternity.
The One that guides me to the truth of who I am.
You are the One that I am.
You are the love that I am.
I am the One that I have been searching for.
I searched for You, and I found myself.

♡

6. PRAYER & DEVOTION

I WANTED TO BE A NUN

I wanted to be a nun
— completely devoted to God.
Away from all the complications
of the world.

But God had a different plan.
He wanted me
to truly understand
why I came and who I am.

So I learned over and over
to look around hidden corners,
so I could wash away
what I am not.

I was angry, and I was sad.
Even devastated
— and at times, I seemed
completely mad.

But that was all
the suffering
that I needed to wash away,
so I could be who I am.

So now, today,
I am not running away
from a complex world,
I thought I saw.

*The hidden corners in my mind
were the complexities that I saw.
It was all my own fear
I needed to free myself from.*

*Not only am I devoted to God now,
I know God is within me
and in everything I perceive.
So now, in grace, I gently walk.*

TURNING TO GOD

When my heart feels heavy
I turn to You.
I ask for Your assistance
to lighten up my heart.

And if my mind is not entangled
in heaviness,
I can easily hear You.
And also, see Your answers
all around me.
In an instant, I am
back with You.

But if I linger too long
and my mind gets entangled,
oh my God,
then it can be hard to hear You
— or to see Your answers.

So God,
in this moment,
right here and now,
I pray.

I pray that when my heart feels heavy,
I will have the strength
to immediately turn to You.
— Before my mind gets further entangled
and tries to find answers,
where there are none.

So God,
here I am.
I am ready to turn to You
immediately,
when my heart feels heavy.
So You, my God
can fill my heart
with light.

I AM YOURS

Here I am.
Oh God, I have tried,
to turn my mind
away from the dark night.

On my knees,
God, hear me, please.
Here I am.
I am Yours.

DEVOTED TO YOU

Love is my destiny.
My one and only goal.
A life in ecstasy.
Merged with my soul.

I walked through fire
to know You, Lord.
You were my one desire
— my only longing in this world.

I heard Your calling
far away from here.
I began falling,
and the world would disappear.

I landed in the dark.
I faced my own shadow.
Beyond it was a spark
that turned into a rainbow.

The colors dispelled the darkness.
The dark had kept me scared.
With true vision, it was harmless.
Now I was finally prepared.

I was ready to know Your love.
I was ready to be like You.
I knew You were my destiny
and only Your love could set me free.

You looked into my eyes.
Everything turned to light.
I finally saw with true sight.
All was gone and all was bright.

THE RETURN

I pray without ceasing.
My life I give to You.
Your love is increasing.
Each moment feels new.

I bathe in Your glory.
With angels, I sing.
Released from all worry
and safe on Your string.

I feel all Your love.
I rest in Your light.
In the Heavens above,
everything is white.

The world has disappeared.
All I see is bright light.
Clean slate now appears.
Everything is quiet.

The prayer of my heart,
was to know only You
— to never feel apart
and to know what is true.

You heard my call.
You brought me Home.
Now I know I'm One with all
— and I was never alone.

THE REMEMBRANCE

In the grace of Your love,
I rise high above.
Merge with the whole
and remember my soul.

LISTEN TO LOVE

*When life seems
hard and unfair
— Pray.*

*When your heart
seems to hurt
— Pray.*

*When tears fall
down your cheeks
— Pray.*

*Prayer brings you
into the vastness of
divine silence.
And in the silence
love always answers.*

*So let us join in prayer
and listen to love.*

It is time to enter the light of love.

PRAYER TO GOD

When darkness falls,
and my heart calls.
For Your strength to come
to bring me back Home.

The pain I feel,
I long to heal.
Down on my knees,
God help me, please.

I close my eyes
to let go of all lies.
These untrue beliefs
make my heart freeze.

God, I turn to You
to show me what is true.
To help me rinse my soul
so I again can feel whole.

With You, I feel safe.
To You, God, I obey.
In Your deep love, I rest.
God, You are the best.

HUMBLENESS

I see only beauty in You.
A reflection of divinity.
Your presence humbles me
and in Your eyes, I see eternity.

Down on my knees.
Washing Your feet.
My heart beats with gratitude
and my love is complete.

In the silent breeze.
God whispers to me,
"You are the Holy One.
Now set yourself free."

Surrendered to You.
My heart feels pure.
I kiss Your hands.
Now I know what is true.

The divinity I see
is a reflection of me.
This presence is myself.
One in eternity.

I reach out to kiss
Your soft cheek.
My life is here with You.
There is nothing more to seek.

FOREVER WITH HIM

I choose a day in His glory.
All else will fade away.
No trace of any worry.
In His arms I will stay.

Soft and so gentle.
A beam of light lifts me up.
The light brings me directly.
High above a mountaintop.

In His glorious essence.
Everything turns to light.
I hear the deep silence.
And my form becomes bright.

I am the light of the world.
One with His magnificence.
To my Home, I have returned.
Forever in His presence.

BACK TO DIVINITY

Right at Your feet,
I humbly weep.

Everything that happened to me
was to set me free.

Free from the insanity,
to bring me back to divinity.

Where I always was meant to be
— resting in the arms of Thee.

LONGING FOR YOU

My heart longs for Your warmth
so I quietly close my eyes.
I feel Your gentle, loving presence
and I embrace Your essence.

Your kind arms hold me tight,
and my head rests on Your chest.
I listen to Your heart sing my song,
and I know it is here I belong.

Oh, this love, this beautiful grace.
All I need to do is close my eyes
to see Your light shining in my mind.
This infinite love cannot be defined.

The thought of You brings me closer.
It opens the gate to Heaven's glory
and bursts my heart wide open
— to eternal love that is unspoken.

TAKE MY HAND

Beloved one,
I am all around you and within you.
At no moment am I absent from you.
Only your choice of thoughts can seem to make it so.

Where could I be where you are not
when you are who I am?

Beloved one,
You are here to love and laugh.
You are here to recognize
that the light you see in Me is yourself.

If you forget and fall into despair,
simply remember to take my hand
and walk with Me.

I will lead you back to the light within you.

A DAILY PRAYER

This day we give to You.
This day we give to love.
Today our hearts are glowing with pure light
— the light radiates to every heart
and awakens the whole world to Your love.

This day we remember that we are all One
— One with You and eternally Yours.
Today we know there is nothing more to do.
Today we know our Holiness.

The journey is over, and we remember it was all a dream.
In heartfelt laughter, we join together,
and we finally remember that we never left You.
In Your arms, we now rest forever,
knowing that we are awake.

Today it is all complete.

MY BELOVED JESUS

In my Holiness I walk with You,
certain and clear of my path.
Gently my feet touch the ground,
and I feel the earth below me.

My heart beats to the rhythm of Your grace
and my eyes solely see Your glory.
The sun touches my face
and lovingly warms up my skin.

I feel the wind blowing though my hair
and washing away my tears of gratitude.
Your soft and calm hand is holding my hand,
and I follow You in every step that I take.

You are here beside me,
and together we are gently walking Home.
You are here to remind me we are One.
And I am here only to listen to You
— and to follow You to the end of time.
Into the timeless eternity that is our true Home
and our true nature.

My beloved Brother,
lead me to my heart
and show me that it glows like Yours
— glows like the brightest star in the Heavens above.
I trust You
I Love You
Thank You

THANK YOU

I thank You for Your unconditional love for me.
I thank You for Your unwavering faith in me.
I thank You for all Your gifts to me.
I thank You for filling my heart and mind with the truth.
I thank You for always listening to me.
I thank You for guiding me.
I thank You for always being here for me.
I thank You for Your endless patience with me.
I thank You for never giving up on me.
I thank You for consistently calling me Home.
I thank You for opening my heart to receive Your love.
I thank You for opening my eyes to see You in everything I see.
I thank You for opening my ears to hear only Your voice.
I lay humble by Your feet to be at Your service.
In deep honor and gratitude, I give myself to You,
knowing that my will and Yours are One.

EVERY DAY'S MISSION

I am the love I see in you.
You are the love you see in me.
As One we will always be
— and this realization will set us free.

This is our mission today and every day
— to remember the One love.

GOD IS

God appears in everyone and everything.
There is nowhere He is not ever-present.

He is the spark of light within everyone you meet.
He is the vast presence in everything you see.

If you simply remember this,
you will not get falsely entangled
during your short stay here,

but instead spread His spark
and lift this realm up to the Heavens.

So merge with Him my beloved.

Let us be what He is, because only that is true.

A PRAYER TO MY FATHER

Beloved Father
Whatever You want me to do, I am here for You.
I give You my eyes to see.
I give You my mouth to speak.
I give You my ears to hear.
I give You my feet to walk.
I give You my arms to hug.
I give You my heart to beat.
I give You my breath to breathe.
I give You my life to live.

Father, I know my will and Yours are one.

PART II, QUOTES

1. *WISDOM*

In the absence of who I thought I was, I meet my true self.

Whatever you say or do, it can never change my love for you.

Nothing can be but in perfect order and completely orchestrated by the One who loves you unconditionally.

The changelessness of the truth is what makes it real.

Nothing is impossible unless you believe it is.

*True vision is not of the body's eyes,
but is born in the faith of a believer with a pure heart.*

Only wrong thinking causes suffering. You suffer because you cling onto something or reject something. Suffering is a sign of unwillingness to surrender to what IS. An unwillingness to surrender to the present moment. Suffering is only in the mind. It is only imagined, and it has no reality whatsoever. It is unnatural and can be released by looking at what it is that you are clinging to and/or rejecting.

Truth and wisdom can only be found in inner silence.

It is impossible to joyfully play
if you are trying to control the direction of the game.

When you follow the Holy Spirit's guidance,
everything in your life becomes as easy as breathing.

There is nothing to learn for the one that is already complete.
However, there is seemingly a lot to unlearn to realize the completion.

Only the truth can be shared.
Anything else leads you nowhere.

*When the light comes near,
fear begins to disappear.*

*Love does not need anything or anyone as it is complete,
just being itself.*

It is when your deepest darkness hits you that you have the biggest opportunity to remember your true self. The darkness is there to push you from the edge where you thought you had found safety in the world. It pushes you out of your illusionary comfort zone to wake you up. True safety lies only in God and in seeing this you will set yourself free. Only in God can you know yourself, and only in God do you have eternal safety.

When you begin seeing the false as false,
you are simultaneously beginning to see the truth.

Just relax! Enjoy the show and let your true being flow.

Love gives without expectations.
Love gives without exceptions.

You are forever innocent, and I see you.

*You are a masterpiece, eternal and complete.
So why are you looking for more?*

*No one sees the same world. Everyone sees through a veil of a belief system made up of unreliable memories of past experiences. The whole cosmos is basically a projected screen of what we believe about ourselves; and beliefs are decisions in the mind made up by how we have analyzed situations we seemingly have experienced. And because we see through a made-up veil of beliefs, we do not see the truth. The veil is distorting our sight and blocking us from seeing clearly. The whole perceptual world is completely distorted, and is the reason why we cannot join in what we perceive. It is like the famous story of the five blind men touching different parts of an elephant. All five describe the elephant completely differently. This is how we 'see'. We are basically blind! How can we know that our brother sees the same kind of blue sky as we see? We cannot know. Only in the truth can we truly join, and only the truth can be shared, as it is completely consistent. The truth will be revealed when perception ceases to exist; when we have released ourselves from all our beliefs and we see only love — a life in complete peace, where everything is forgiven, and we dance in joy into eternity. Your part is to release yourself from the veil and return to Heaven. When you see with the eyes of God, you see God
in everything and everyone.*

Life is a love affair with God, if we really understood it.

*You are simply just an actor. Play your part with love and kindness.
Then your movie will be beautiful.*

*Let everything be exactly as it is.
Let the wind blow wherever it will.
Let the waves of the ocean go wherever they will.
Let the birds fly wherever they will.
Do not try to disturb or direct anything.
Your release from attachments to this world
lies simply in observing and letting everything be
exactly as it is without wanting, needing or judging.
Simply lay back, smile at it all and rest in the grace of God.
Your part is that simple.*

The pathway of a mystic is a direct experience with the divine.

*Turning deep within, you will realize that there can only be one reality.
Reality cannot be split into parts. Reality is changeless and eternal.
Nothing real can ever change. All forms of this world are constantly moving towards distortion. They come from nothing, and they will return to nothing.
Including the body you believe that you are. Only that which is changeless and real has always been and will always be. And that has no form!
That truth is within you. That truth IS you! Turn deep within, way past thoughts and beliefs about something other than the truth.
The truth is waiting for you to remember, to remember who you are. This is your only function while you believe that you are in this world.*

*When you are ready, a door to your next assignment will open automatically.
Do not doubt yourself, and do not doubt that which is shown to you is for you.
It is always for you. You can choose to resist life, and therefore you will seem to suffer. Or you can welcome life and simply be happy now! Remember that you are never alone. I will walk with you into eternity. Be a happy learner and return Home in joy! I love you forever and ever.*

You cannot directly see the light in you, but you can see your light through your brother. This is how you see yourself. You see your own light glowing through your brother. Your brother is yourself, reflecting back at you what you believe about yourself. Your brother is always pointing you towards your true self. You cannot see the illusionary darkness directly in you. But your brother will point you to the darkness that is blocking your light, so you can release yourself from it. It is out of love and kindness that you perceive darkness in a brother.

It is your own darkness. Not your brother's! Your brother is merely showing you your beliefs that are blocking your light. All darkness is just blocks and ego beliefs, and they are completely untrue. You need your brother to unwind from the belief in the dream of duality. Darkness and light cannot coexist.

The world is made up of the ego, and it is a world of duality. The ego uses it to keep you asleep, but the light can use it to point you to the truth. And there can only be One truth. Multiple truths are impossible. You need your brother to show you who you are, and who you are not. You need your brother to remind you that you are One; that you are the light, and that you are One with him. You need your brother to remind you that you are dreaming and that your part is to wake up. The journey to awakening gets much easier when you acknowledge that God is calling you Home through your brother. Your brother is your gift to lead you Home. You brother has been sent to you by God to show you that you are One love; that you are One eternal light. You will reach God. It is inevitable. Purification is needed first. Forgiveness is the purification.

When you realize that you do not know anything about what you
thought you knew, then you are beginning to know something.

True wisdom can only be experienced in a mind of the one who has let go of all
attachments, desires and judgments. Holding onto anything of the world will
block true wisdom. True wisdom can only be experienced in the eyes of the pure
and innocent. The one who thinks only with God is truly free. Only when one has
renounced all that is false, can one truly live.

Before you will know true love, you will experience your heart break a thousand
times into a thousand pieces.

The one that only speaks, thinks and acts from a pure heart,
is simply happy.

Anything you cannot take with you when you lay aside the body has no value whatsoever.

When you try to exclude yourself from the world and from your brothers, you actually want to be in control. This might seem very confusing and hard to understand, and that is exactly where the sneaky ego wants you to be — in a state of confusion. Nothing here is what it seems. When you feel excluded, you are only upset because you are not in control; so you place yourself 'outside' (exclude yourself) to try to control the situation — to try to control your life. You are in an 'I know better' mode, and in that state, you actually think you are in competition with God. The ego feeds on being in control, and you feed the ego by believing in it. Wanting to be in control is an authority problem. Wanting to be separated from your brothers and from God is an authority problem. The feeling of exclusion is an authority problem, but the ego tries to make you feel like a victim to hide the core issue. The victim role keeps the ego's game going on and on by projecting the belief in victimization (exclusion) onto the world; and the underlying issue is kept hidden in that way instead of being exposed.
Feeling like a victim and feeling excluded are basically arrogant!
But when the truth gets exposed, the ego will be dissolved in the light. When you realize that you are One with your brothers and One with God, you will know that the will of God is your will as well, and you will be free. Remember you are loved beyond measure, and God awaits patiently on your homecoming. You are never excluded, nor are you a victim.
You are eternally included, complete, perfect and forever loved.

When you decide to go for the truth, remember that you cannot fail.

Only the truth can be shared. It is impossible to share something that will not last forever. What is temporal and limited cannot be shared. How could you give something that eventually will decay? A true gift can only be eternal. Therefore, only the truth can be shared.

God is found in the absence of anything you can grab onto.

Your mind is extremely powerful.
Use it only to extend the love of God,
and you will realize that love is all that you are.

*Everything that seems to happen to you, without exception, is a blessing.
It is God kissing your forehead to let you know that you are so loved.
Only when you resist what life is giving you, you seem to suffer. But remember
that suffering is only in your mind. It has no reality whatsoever. You only
suffer because you choose to believe that life is against you; that God is against
you. When you begin to see that everything is a gift to help you unwind from
your beliefs, your life will become like a dance. You will see everything as a
miracle. Be a happy learner and dance with life. Dance with God.*

*The happy dream is simply a life without the ego ruling.
It is a life where you are awake, and the Spirit in you is ruling.*

*The ego's game is to struggle and survive,
but Spirit simply just enjoys life.*

*All is light.
I am that.
The rest is a dream.*

Choosing peace is your biggest contribution to the whole universe.

*Nothing can keep us apart, except thoughts about separateness.
And those are just that — thoughts.*

*This world is just an experiment to see if you can wake up
and walk out if it.*

*In the stillness of your heart,
you will find the answer to what you are seeking.*

You were never born, and you will never die.

Nothing you experience is not for you! Everything you experience is God loving you! It is only in the ego's judgments that some situations are good and some are bad. Practice reaching a state of mind where everything is equally acceptable. When you reach a state of mind without judgments, your mind will rest in the love of God. You will experience true freedom. Question everything that you value or devalue. Both are blocks to the awareness of the truth. Everything is perfect as it is. This moment is perfect. This moment is all that is.

Forgiveness is the ticket to Heaven.

The truth of you is a perfect creation — complete, loving and kind, and at peace forever in the heart of God.

With the death of the false self lies the birth of true wisdom.

The way you see yourself is the way you will act in the world — and the way you will see your brothers and sisters, as they are mirrors of your mind. So, if you see yourself as incomplete and lacking, you will see everyone and everything in the same way. If you see yourself as loving, peaceful and complete, you will see the same in everything and everyone you meet — or even think of. It is simply your choice of how you want to be and how you want to see the world. It all comes down to changing your mind about yourself.

The silent mind is changeless and cannot be disturbed. The busy mind changes constantly and is totally disturbed. In truth you are the silent mind, but you've been believing that you are the busy mind. The only way to be silent is to let go of all the noise that is blocking the awareness of your true identity.
You are not your thoughts. You are beyond thinking.

In the silence, you will remember your true self.
Be still and know.

This whole world is only mental. It is made up by thoughts of likes and dislikes. It is an illusionary scenario made of opposites. When you truthfully look within, you know intuitively that truth can have no opposites. Truth can only be One. So, a world of differences and opposites can never be real. It only appears to be so because of the power of thoughts and beliefs. It is possible to perceive only Oneness — to see only the truth. It takes practice, willingness and consistency to unwind from what is false. Returning to the truth is actually inevitable! It seems as if it takes time to return to the truth, but time is a trick and a part of the illusion. Truth is a choice at this moment, and that choice is up to you. The only time to choose the truth is now. There is only now! Choose right now to return to the truth — to love, to Oneness and rest in the peace of God forever.

The answer is always love.

Drop that which is not permanent and let yourself awaken to the infinite.

Wherever you go and whatever you do, do not plant anything but love. Always come with love and always leave with love. Always do everything with love. This is how you will wash away anything in you that is blocking love. What you give, you give to yourself. What you extend, you will become. And what you are in truth is love.

Truth can be hidden behind the illusion, but it can never be lost. The way back to the remembrance of the truth is to realize that you are not a figure in the dream, but the dreamer of the dream. And if you go even deeper, you will realize that there never was a dream and you never left God.

You are the light that can dispel the fear and realize that only love is real.

The ego's purpose is to collect stuff and be right about everything. It wants things in a certain way to be satisfied. It wants to make itself real by deluding you into thinking that you can find safety in things and people. Its mission is to get more. Just more. No matter what it is. Its purpose is to make the world it made up seem real. The ego only takes and never gives. If the ego 'gives' it is always to get something back. The ego collects things to try to build something out of nothing — to make you believe that it can keep you safe and make you happy. Everything the ego thinks is basically absolutely meaningless. It is never going to get you anywhere near what you in truth are searching for. Spirit on the other hand is changeless, eternal, complete and in need of nothing. Spirit knows only what is true and real. Spirit gives and gives and gives. Spirit is love, and ego is fear. If we saw this very clearly, we would drop the ego thinking immediately like a hot potato. The choice between love and fear is in your mind. Everything is in your mind. Now is the time to choose — the choice is between Spirit or ego. It is actually that simple! There will come a point where you will only hear one voice, and you will know that you are Spirit, and the false idea of separation will be gone.

Just go for it!!! Follow your heart and don't look back.

With a consistent focus on letting go of the false self, your true self will dawn upon you. And from that instant, all you will know is the truth. Nothing will disturb you. Nothing will have any effect on you. Only the truth will remain in your Holy mind, and you will be at peace forever. That is your true nature. That is your true self.

Fear is always a call for love — for God, but often gets played out by trying to run away from love or push love away. Desire is simply a sign that you are longing for love — for God. Life is all about remembering love.

In silence, God is.

2. FREEDOM

Life is like a symphony. Everyone plays their part and comes into our lives at the perfect time. Some instruments play a long part, and other's parts are short. Some instruments play through the whole symphony. Everything is in divine order, and thankfully we do not have to control the symphony. We do not have to have any thought about how it sounds. Our part is to enjoy it, dance to it and sing to it. Be like a feather in the wind, dancing to the universal symphony.

Walk with me now. The past is not here, and neither is tomorrow.

Hidden under your biggest fear is your release from it. I am here to help you walk through it. Trust in me and take my hand.

To know God requires letting go of everything you think you know and think you have.

When you are willing to sink into the ocean instead of grasping the water to try to swim, you will realize that you can float.

In complete forgiveness lies true freedom.

You can learn by studying, but true understanding can only come from a real experience. Intellect does not bring you to the truth. Only by letting go of the belief that you know anything can you begin to really know something. The one who has become humble in his heart has begun to truly understand. Prayer is a way to humble your heart. True prayer asks for nothing. It only asks for what already IS. True prayer asks for help to wash away the false, so the truth can be revealed. It asks for the remembrance of what already IS, always was and always will be. There can truly only be one true prayer and that prayer is for knowing who you are! That knowing will come as an experience when you are ready, and in the experience all questions and all searching will dissolve. The peace of God will dawn on you, and all will be still — all will be blissful.

I was born the instant I finally loved everything I once feared.

You are not the one who feels fear, anxiety, loss, pain or suffering. The truth of you is Spirit, and Spirit is purely love. All else is an illusion you have trained your mind to believe in. You have the power to unwind from these beliefs and remember the truth of who you are. It takes willingness and unwavering commitment. What more than knowing who you are can be important here? Happy awakening to love.

Contentment lies in surrendering to the Will of God, and in acknowledging that His Will and yours are one.

Gratitude can bring you back into a state of peace. When you mistakenly have negative thoughts, drop them immediately and turn your mind towards thoughts of gratitude. Those thoughts can be as simple as thankfulness for having woken up this morning to another beautiful day of opportunities to give.

True freedom is a state of mind that can be experienced when all attachments and judgments have been released.

You can either choose to be in the center of your being, completely calm and at peace — like in the quiet center of a tornado, or you can choose to be outside the center and be yearning for peace.

Be equally grateful for what has been given you, as for what seemingly has been denied you. They are the same. Both are your gifts.

The wind erased all obstacles to the silence, and everything turned to peace.

No matter how much you try to make something happen or avoid something happening, only what is meant to happen will happen. You are not in charge of anything. But you are loved beyond measure by the One who is. The pain you sometimes feel is only your resistance to this fact. Everything that life brings to you is what is the most loving and the most helpful for your awakening. It is God's love pointing you to the truth of who you are. It is God calling you Home.

*Do not take anything in this world seriously, nor personally.
Your freedom lies in this practice.*

*In stillness you will hear His answer. In stillness you will know His love.
In the stillness of this Holy instant lies the answer you are searching for.
Be still and listen. In the vastness of this Holy instant lies the grace of God.*

*Seek only for that which is changeless.
Everything else will eventually fade away.*

All you can ever lose is fear, and fear is completely unreal. When you realize this, you will no longer be afraid of letting go. What you truly want to have can never be lost — and that is love. You were created by your loving Father, and what you are in truth, which is love, can never be lost. You are One with your Father, and anything that does not share this Oneness with Him, is only fear — and completely unreal. Remember that you are love and nothing can touch the eternal and changeless.

Once you know your Oneness with God, your true vision will appear, and you will see God in everyone.

The door will automatically open up when you are ready. You cannot force the door to open, nor can you close it again. When you are ready for your next step, the door will open up by itself. And God will wait patiently for you to enter.

A path that doesn't lead to love, joy and peace, is simply an illusion.

Try not to resist change in your life. All changes are perfectly orchestrated by the One in charge and who loves you unconditionally. You cannot know how the puzzle is supposed to look. But be sure that you are a very important piece in the whole picture — as the puzzle would be incomplete without you. You cannot possibly see the whole picture from your point of view. Have faith and trust! Everything is going to fall into place, and your part is essential. When all has fallen into place, everything will be One, whole and perfectly complete. The Will of God is for you to remember your Oneness with Him — and have eternal peace and happiness. Your part is to surrender and simply just be. Be like a feather in the wind and let yourself be carried, where God would have you be.

The biggest prayer you can say is, Thank You.

The one who has realized that true love can only be experienced in a complete devotion to God, has found the answer to his prayers.

You can try to run from Me. You can try to hide from Me. You can try to hate Me and you can try to fear Me. But deep within I am everything you are yearning for. Eventually you will realize that I am your only goal. You will then see that we are the same, and you will realize that you were searching for yourself.

There is One life, and it is forever.

No amount of darkness can dispel the light.
But even a tiny candle can dispel the darkness.

Look gently deep inside. Anything you identify with will limit you.
As long as you hold onto any roles or concepts, you will not find the consistent peace and eternal love that you are searching for. Roles and concepts block the truth from your awareness. By letting go of what you are not, you will remember who you are.

Let what is untrue be undone, so the light can shine undisrupted forever and ever.

Accept everyone as they are and love them.

In the absence of fear of death and fear of life, lies the truth of who you are.
It can be experienced as a fire of joy, an explosion of love, as complete silence, or as a combination of it all.

*The ones that push your buttons the most are your greatest gifts from God.
They show you exactly the blocks in your mind that need to be released
— so you can remember who you are.*

*Beyond the blocks to love's presence shines your eternal light — bright and pure
and waiting for you to recognize it.*

*When all questions have ceased to be, one will rest in the stillness of God's grace,
unaware of anything but the knowing of the true self.*

*No matter what life brings you, the truth of you can never be affected.
You are and will always be a beautiful bright light, unconditionally loved and
unbound by anything of this world. Life experiences are there only to bring you
back into the awareness of the truth of who you are. May your life be a beautiful
experience, filled with strength, love, happiness and peace.*

Stop pretending to be small. Your magnificence is needed!

I searched for love everywhere I could think of, but I never found it anywhere. When I had given up searching and looked within, I finally realized that all this time, it was love that had been searching for itself. So I ended the searching. I had finally found myself.

When a candle is lit in the dark, the darkness vanishes. Light your candle and transform the darkness into light. Let there be light.

Simple living is the most giving. The closer you come to God, the simpler you become. Only the ego is complex. God is simple.

Only resistance to what IS brings you pain. Peace is found in total acceptance of what IS in this moment. Be grateful for everything God gives you. Let go of desires for anything other than what is. Your freedom lies in this.

You are absolute perfection. It's only your thoughts about yourself that need to change.

Do not get lost in concepts. You are beyond all concepts. You are the dreamer of the dream. Do not identify with the character you play. You are not the character. Question all your beliefs. Be totally honest. Nothing can be kept hidden, or it will keep you asleep and identified with the role you play. Everything has to be brought into the light. In the light, you will see the dream for what it is. Just totally unreal. Forgive until you know there is nothing to forgive. Align with the Kingdom of Heaven. Merge with the love of God. Be the light of truth. Just Be.

Suffering is a sign that you have chosen to believe your thoughts, and your choice is blocking you from the truth. Question every belief that you have and see them for what they are — untrue. Then let them go. Set yourself free from wrong thinking. Take responsibility for your state of mind. Your happiness lies in it.

You cannot see innocence in anyone nor yourself before you fully desire it. Desiring to see only innocence is the first step towards forgiveness. It is a step towards your freedom.

No problem is real, and the one who thinks there is a problem, is not real either.

When you can look at yourself in a mirror and see only love, you will see God.

Remember that you came for the salvation of the world. You came to remember who you are. That is all that this world is for. The world you perceive is in your mind. What you believe you perceive. Forgive and remember the love that you are. When you choose to look within is up to you, but the realization of your true self is inevitable. You can choose to wait for lifetimes, but the truth is available now! Your unwavering willingness is needed to forgive everything you believe in, and to forgive your brother — who is yourself. When you desire peace above all else, the opportunities you need to unwind from what is blocking your peace will be given to you. It will sometimes seem as if life is against you. But life is always for you. Do not doubt this! What life brings to you IS your gift to let go of the blocks to peace and love. You can choose peace now and fill your heart up with love, so the love of God can flow out from your heart and onto the whole world. Let true love flow and remember that you came for the salvation of the world. It is time to return to innocence.

Remember you are dreaming!
There is no need to take anything seriously here.

Glow and Grow!

When you step back and let God lead the way, you are embracing the flow of life. That and only that will bring you peace of mind.

The world you see is only a reflection of your state of mind. Do you see beauty and love? Then that is your state of mind. Do you see fear and pain? Then that is your state of mind. The most wonderful thing is that you can choose your state of mind by choosing your thoughts. Choose beautiful and loving thoughts, thoughts you think with God, and you will see a paradise before your eyes. Or choose fearful thoughts, thoughts of the ego, and you basically will see hell. What do you want to see? How do you want to feel? You will perceive what you believe. And by the way, only loving thoughts are real.

Heaven awaits on your returning Home
— and to realize that you were never alone.

The only control you have, is of your thoughts. It is only with your thoughts that you can change anything. When you react to a brother's words or actions you are reacting to your own thoughts about what he says or does.
Your brother is only showing you your own thoughts and beliefs.
Any reaction to a brother is pointing you to a part in you that needs to be healed. This whole world is for you to be released from your thoughts and beliefs. You can choose healing now, or you can choose to keep on believing in your illusionary thoughts and beliefs - and by choosing the illusion, you are only delaying yourself. Your brother and this whole world is your gift to transcend the unreal and to leap into true and eternal Happiness. This world is only a dream, and you can choose to wake up now!

Never give up!!! If it feels expanding and it lifts you up then keep on going. The universal plan for you is much more amazing than you can ever imagine.

That which will never disappear is the only true reality. Everything you seemingly perceive 'outside' yourself will disappear. Even your body will eventually cease to exist. The only thing that is still here when all else is gone, is the truth. It is the true love that you are. Within you is perfect love, eternal and changeless. Anything other than that has no reality whatsoever. Turn within and find that which never disappears and is far too vast to be described with words. Find your true identity in the love of God. Every moment of your life is just for that. Life is very simple. Turn within and know Thyself.

Everything you do is universal. So, all thoughts of personal investments or responsibilities are unnecessary in anything you do. Everything is done by Spirit. The One universal Spirit - which is the truth of you! It is impossible that anything can go wrong. Everything is always exactly as it is supposed to be. This thought, if truly believed, will bring you into a restful state of love, peace, joy and freedom.

When I allowed myself to accept God's infinite love pouring down on me and embracing me, I experienced that this love was so overwhelming that all I could do was to give it away. Then I experienced that I kept on being filled up with God's love. The more I gave away, the more I felt the love. I saw that true love is eternal, changeless and all-inclusive. By giving love away, I realized that I am this love. I am the love of God.

Nothing is capable of disturbing your peace except false thoughts. Choose true thoughts and be at peace forever. Thoughts that bring you calmness and happiness, and make you want to happily share them with the whole world, are your true thoughts. These thoughts are the only ones that truly can be shared. They remind you of your true self. Which is love.
True thoughts bring peace in your mind and love in your heart.

*Simply take the first step and the path to infinite love
will be shown to you by itself.*

Anything or anyone you desire more than peace and love will keep you from knowing who you are. Step back and ask yourself what you are holding onto. What do you value more than peace and love? Only by renouncing everything you believe you need more than peace and love, will you come to know your true self. You will know that you ARE peace and love. Everything else is simply a poor substitute for the truth.

*It is impossible to add something to perfection.
So seeking something to add to you is simply silly.*

3. ETERNITY

The proper use of time is for undoing the belief in it.

There is no beginning, nor is there an ending.
There is only true love in this Holy instant.

May this Holy instant of love shine from your soul
and may the love of God embrace your beautiful heart forever.

There is a melody that was before time was.
It plays softly without ceasing.
In silence you can hear it playing your song.
The song that is calling you Home.

*Time is but a construct made to keep you from
remembering the divine love that you are.*

*Your true self can never be touched by anything external. No matter what seems
to happen, it will always remain the same — changeless and eternal.*

*The past is an interpretation. The future is a hypothetical based on an
interpretation of the past. Both past and future are thoughts based on
interpretation of the past and have nothing to do with reality whatsoever.
Reality is only now.*

*If you believe that you are a body, you believe you are limited. This is not true.
If you believe that you are Spirit, you believe that you are limitless.
This is completely true.*

It is time to unwind from the illusion of time.

Make this glorious moment so filled with love that nothing else can touch it.

Your part is simply to stay in the not knowing and have faith.
The not knowing is completely absent of thoughts of the past and the future.
The not knowing is a gateway into union with God.

Try not to interfere. Everything is planned exactly in your favor.
Even though it sometimes seems as if your life is falling apart, there is a divine order behind everything. Your part is only to stay calm, breathe and let go of fear. Know that you are completely safe and unconditionally loved
by the divine orchestrator.

Living in the moment with no thoughts of what was or what is to come, is a life completely given over to joyful miracles.

You never left Home. You never left God. And God never left you!

I crossed the bridge to eternity, and I never looked back.

Everything of this world is temporary. Do not get caught up in anything that does not last. When you think you have obtained what you believe you want, you will be afraid of losing it again. Nothing of this world will ever give you what your heart truly longs for. Covered up by everything you think you want, is what you really long for. And that is true love. You are actually longing to remember who you truly are. And that is love. You are love.

The solution to any problem you perceive cannot be resolved in time. If you believe that things will get better in time, you are removing yourself from the solution to every seeming problem you perceive. You are basically removing yourself from the only reality there is. The now! The Holy instant — the answer! The solution to any seeming problem can only be given in the stillness of God. God has nothing to do with time. God does not know of time! The ego made up time to distract you from the truth, and the ego has no real solution to offer you — as it isn't real. No matter how much you try, you will never find any answers in time. It is impossible to find an answer in an illusion. Trying to find an answer in a world of illusions to your seeming problems will only entangle you deeper into the belief that there is a real problem, that there is time, and that there is a world outside yourself. Trying to find a solution in the illusion indicates that you believe that you have a real problem, and you believe there is a world outside yourself that can give you something; a world that can make you happy. This belief makes you dependent on something outside of yourself to be happy. But happiness is within you! Bringing all your seeming problems to the Holy Spirit, who is the voice for God within you, is where the answer is given. And He gives you the answer immediately! The answer is closer than your breath. The answer is before time was, and can only be experienced in the stillness of the Holy instant — where the truth of you abides. You already have the answer to everything, Beloved One. Your happiness can only be found in this moment. In the Holy instant, all questions dissolve, and only the truth remains. The Holy instant is the answer! Be still, listen and you will hear the voice of God calling you out of the world and back into Oneness with Him.
You are perfect, eternal and complete. And you have no problems!!!
The one who knows he is complete cannot perceive any lack or problems.
Love and blessings to you, Holy One.

This everlasting moment is glorious in the light of love.

Nothing in this world will ever give you satisfaction. Only God suffices. Anything else will never bring you happiness and will eventually fall away. Seek only the eternal. Seek only God. God is all there is.

The past is simply an unreliable memory that does not exist. The future is an unreliable memory projected into an anticipated future that does not exist either. Only this Holy instant is real. Only the now IS. It is as simple as that! Happy Holy instant.

Now is the time to turn towards the sun and let yourself bloom.

Surrender now and set yourself free. The present moment is your key.

The past and the future are only thoughts.

There is no time but now.

When you step back and let God lead the way, you are embracing the flow of life. That and only that will bring you peace of mind.

Everything you want from this world will eventually fade to nothing. That is the reason why nothing in this world can bring you consistent happiness. It is impossible to find consistency in the inconsistent. Therefore, seek only for that which is changeless and eternal. In that you will find true happiness. In that you will find yourself.

When you look through the eyes of the ego, images and differences seem to exist. When you look at the ego with the Spirit, the ego ceases to exist — and all will be experienced as One.

The truth can only be recognized when you realize the unreality of the dreamworld. The world is a dream, and you are dreaming it. When you take the dream seriously you have mistakenly taken the ego to be real. Look with the Spirit and you will know yourself. You are Spirit.

Time is just a thought. You try to make it real by believing in it, but in truth, there is no time, no past, and no future. It is all just a thought. Only the present moment is true. The present moment is completely absent of false thoughts, and the present moment has nothing to do with time whatsoever. The present moment is a state of mind, and it is the answer to every seeming problem you believe you have — as everything untrue vanishes in the vastness of it. In the absence of all that is false — all thoughts that do not bring you peace, the present moment is experienced as a state of complete bliss. It is love, peace, and happiness. It is the experience of who you are in truth.
It is a deep realization that all is One.

There has never been a moment where you have not been complete and perfect.

It only takes an instant to love completely.

We are only imagining that we are bound by a world and a body. In truth we are already completely free, and far beyond what we seem to see.

There is no life apart from union with God.

When you know without any doubt that you are changeless and eternal, nothing will have the power to bother you. You will be like the sky. The sky stays the same and is never affected by the weather or the clouds passing by.
In your certainty, you will know that all things will pass, and that you are the vast eternal that is far beyond what words can describe.
You are that which always IS.

God can only be known in the now.

Be willing to die to time and be reborn in this moment. Only now can the love of God be experienced. There is no life apart from this moment. Life is only now.

God is present in every moment. God is never absent. That is a fact. Only a false thought can mislead you into believing something other than that fact. A true thought can instantly bring you back to the awareness of God's presence. God is here now!

Lay your heart in the hands of God and let go. Be willing to play your part in the divine symphony by only following His directions. A divine symphony needs clean and pure notes.

Before time was, you were.

I am now.
Yesterday, I am not.
Neither am I tomorrow.
Only now, I am.

The meaning of life is life itself. It is right here within you.
It is the beautiful you! You cannot find any meaning in anything you perceive outside of yourself, because there is nothing outside of you. Only this living moment is all meaningful, because it is all there is. Life is now, and only now.
You are life itself. You are the meaning of life.
Life is a state of mind, and you are a Holy mind.

Happiness is found in the absence of thoughts of the past and the future — in the absence of what does not exist. Happiness is here now.

What is not needed for your remembrance of Heaven will fall away. Trust and let it be so. Holding on to what is not helpful will keep you away from the awareness that you are already Home, safe in the arms of your Father.

There is nothing joyful about the thought of time. But the thought of timelessness is all joyful, and indeed a truthful thought.

Take a leap of faith. All you can lose is fear.
There is no reason to wait. The Holy instant is here waiting for you to enter into eternity. Trust in Me and take My hand. I am here to walk with you and guide you through it all. And my love, I will never let you go.
I love you forever and ever.

The unwinding from the false self is only in the mind. Nothing is really happening, and nothing really did happen at all. All is perfect and always was. You were always the One! And you are loved beyond measure.

Forgiveness is the key to unwind from false perceptions. Forgive, and the gate of Heaven will open up in its sparkling glory. Then walk through the gate with empty hands and the peace of God in your heart.

When the light has burned all the darkness away,
there will be no words left to say.
The journey back home will be complete,
and you can safely push delete.

The best you can do for yourself, and for the whole world, is to be happy. It all begins with you. In this very moment. Each moment is a point of choice. How do you want to feel? The only way to wake up to your true self is to die to the false self. This is mostly experienced as painful. So painful at times that the false self uses the pain to try to convince you that you are on the wrong path. Trust me that this is not so. You can never be on the wrong path. There is only one path and that is walking beside me. You might try to get off by jumping into a ditch, but eventually you will climb back up on the road again when you realize that the ditch is taking you absolutely nowhere. Waking up to your true self is inevitable, and I am with you all the way and into eternity. In the end, you will realize that there was no path and that you always were Home.

No time is needed to realize the truth. Time is a trick! You have the power of God to realize the truth now — in this moment.

Time is but an invention of the mind.

If you simply think of your life as an experience to bring you closer to the presence of love, you will stop taking things seriously. You will smile more frequently, your eyes will glow, and your breath will become lighter. If you happen to begin judging an experience as good or bad, simply remind yourself, that this is only an experience that can bring you back into the presence of love. Nothing is better or worse. And nothing real is actually happening here at all. The truth of you is changeless and eternal. You will always be completely safe and unconditionally loved. Everything here is an experience to point you back to just that. Your mind is very powerful, and it is up to you to choose what you want to experience. Simply choose love and love will be your experience here. Choose love now and share the love. What you give, you always give to yourself as well. Let your experience of life be love.

Get so lost in the moment that you will find your true self.

Even when everything changes around you or seemingly falls apart, you will always stay the same. What eventually will fall away has no value in itself. Only that which is eternal and changeless is valuable, and that is all there truly IS. That is you! Listen to the hush of Heaven calling out your real name. It is calling you out of this world and into eternity. Your true self can only be revealed in the present moment.

Live as if there is only now.
That is the true simplicity of life.
That is the only way to fully live.

The end of uncertainty has come.

Once you have let go of fear of death and fear of life, you can truly live.
A life completely detached from form of any kind, is a life lived in peace.
Peace of God is a state of mind and cannot be compromised with anything
of the world, or you will lose your awareness of what is true and real.

Now is the time to shine your light and pray for peace.

4. COMPLETION

Forgiveness brings the mind into a state of grace.

You are a perfect creation of a loving God. Complete, eternal, and loved unconditionally. When you fully understand this, you will end the search for happiness outside of yourself. You will know you are happiness itself.

Life is but a dream. Your part is just a role. Do not get serious about your role, or anything here. The truth of you is changeless and eternal. Whatever seems to happen here, remember it is really nothing. Play your part, share your love, and follow your bliss.

You are a pure vibrant spark of light, ready to shine onto the whole universe. And the universe is ready for you.

You are a radiant beautiful being. That's it!

There is a door within you that can lead you to the Kingdom of Heaven. Find it. Open it. Walk through it. And stay there.

Oneness is simplicity. Separation is complexity. You can freely choose either one, but only one is true. And only one will bring you peace and happiness.

My heart is illuminated in God's infinite love, and my whole being has melted into His magnificent glory. I rest in His eternal grace forever and ever. God is… and words have ceased to exist.

In any seeming situation that dawns upon you, you always have two options. One is choosing that the situation is for you — and by choosing so, you are choosing love. The other option is choosing that the situation is against you — and by choosing so, you are actually choosing fear. A feeling will always come with your choice, and you know what you have chosen to believe in by tuning into how you are feeling. When you decide — and yes, it IS a decision in the mind, that everything is for you, you feel good. There is a relief in that decision, and a personal responsibility gets lifted off your shoulders. It is the flow of life bringing you a gift, so you can come closer to the remembrance of who you are. Even though the situation might seem extreme, it is still for you, and always an opportunity to bless and love. When you decide that the situation is happening to you — that something is against you, you don't feel good. You feel like a victim, and your mind goes into fear, anger, anxiety, judgments, etc. How do you want to feel? How do you want to spend your day? How do you want to feel right now? It IS actually your choice! No one and nothing outside of you can take your peace away. Only you can choose to do so. There is basically nothing outside of you! Everything you perceive is a projection of your mind and everyone is just playing their part. When you let go of resisting what comes to you and instead begin happily accepting what IS, everything you perceive will begin to shift. You will see a whole new world. When the mind has only love, it perceives only love. And that is what you are in truth.

Deep within you is an obscured treasure. It is the power of your true self. Find it.

Open your eyes and see all the glory God has bestowed upon you.
Let it embrace you from within and let the light shine through you.
And in its magnificence, you will behold the whole universe.

♡

Love God with all your heart, and your heart will be filled with love.

♡

I will walk with you to eternity, and I will never let go of your hand.
Trust in Me, for I will lead you to the Kingdom of Heaven.

♡

Anything that has an opposite, is false.

♡

*If you desire anything other than the peace of God,
you are compromising your whole being.*

♡

Change your mind and you will change the world.

♡

Your happiness can make the whole world smile. Your part is only to let go of everything in your mind that does not bring a smile to your face. Change your mind, and you will see a beautiful world smiling back at you.

♡

You can transcend the whole perceptual world now by listening only to the loving hymns of Heaven. This is the recipe for consistent happiness.

♡

If you would see the beauty that I see in you, you would weep recognizing your divinity. You would immediately melt into God's glory, and your heart would expand with so much love and compassion that you would see light stream out of you. With your light you can lighten up the whole universe. Your only function is to accept your divine Oneness with God.

♡

Obstacles to love's presence are just thoughts in your mind that trick you into believing that you are not already whole. In truth there are no obstacles. Obstacles are simply just imagined. You are already whole; you always were whole; and you will always be whole. Right now, you are complete! And there is nothing you can do, think or say that can ever change that fact. End the belief in obstacles to love's presence and embrace your wholeness now!
Thank you for your devotion to awakening.

This life experience is all about giving — freely giving. Giving without expectations. Giving from your heart. What you give you become. Life is about being in service to what is true, and being in true service will lift you up into the remembrance of your true self. So be a demonstration of what you want to experience in your life. Be who you are in truth! That and only that will bring you the happiness you are seeking. You have the power to live the most amazing life you can imagine! It is all up to you! Happiness is here now!

In the absence of all meaningless mind chatter, you can hear the gentle voice of Spirit calling you out of the world. Be still, listen and follow.
I am with you all the way.

*No amount of darkness can ever blow out the light from a candle.
The candle will always light up the darkness, no matter the size of the candle.
The light within you can never vanish, as it is who you are.
You can dispel the darkness by simply being who you truly are.
And only you can let your light shine.*

♡

*Eventually, you will reach a point where all questions have fallen away,
and your mind rests in a state of not knowing anything of this world.
In that realization, true knowing will dawn on you.
Oneness with God will wash over you. And when Oneness is
a consistent experience, questions will cease to arise.*

♡

*You will remain in poverty until you know your true self.
Only the One who knows himself, knows the riches of the Kingdom.
And only in the Kingdom of Heaven can abundance be experienced.*

♡

The whole cosmos is you!

♡

When what you do warms your heart and brings you joy,
then you have found your purpose.

♡

You will realize that you have everything
when you peacefully can give up everything.

♡

The light of truth just scooped me up,
and I went all the way to the top.

♡

You know in your heart when you have chosen a miracle.
A miracle is basically peace of mind.

Choosing peace is your biggest contribution to the whole universe.

Express only the message of truth straight from your heart
and everything you will perceive will be love.

Giving is living. You can only give what you are.
All that you are is love.
So, love is all that you can truly give.

May the light of truth shine through you now
and extend to the whole universe.

When you see love in the eyes of everyone you meet,
you will have found love within yourself.

♡

The ego's game is to struggle and survive.
But Spirit simply just enjoys life.

♡

You are a universal love-tool. A channel of the power of love. It is through you that love can shine in this world. It is through you that love can extend in this world. It is the extension of love through you that transcends this world into the truth. By being love, everything transforms into love. By accepting who you are, all will be love.

♡

See pleasure and pain in the world as the same. Both are illusions.

♡

By letting go of desires for anything in the world,
you will feel contentment. You will soar in a state of bliss,
knowing the truth of who you are.

♡

Sprinkle your fairy dust wherever you go
and see how magically your life will flow.

♡

Rejecting God's Will is the same as denying yourself happiness.

♡

In true giving lies release from the belief in lack. Give freely without expectations.
Give from the heart. Give like God gives. Be an instrument of giving.
Be an instrument of peace. Be an instrument of love. Be an instrument of joy.
A smile is also a beautiful gift.

Happy is the one who has renounced all attachments and desires.
He is in need of nothing, as he knows he is already complete.
He knows he is not just a drop in the ocean — but the whole ocean.

Learn kindness from the one you perceive as unkind.
Learn compassion from the one you perceive as indifferent.
Learn patience from the one you perceive as impatient.
Learn trust from the one you perceive as untrustworthy.
Love the one you perceive as unloving.
Everyone has a lesson for you to learn so you can remember your true identity. Everyone is playing their part perfectly because you are so unconditionally loved.

To be in service to God, to extend His love no matter what you seem to be doing, is the most beautiful way to live. It is the only way to truly live. And it will eventually bring you into a state of grace. Simply do everything in His love, and love will be your only experience. What you give, you give to yourself. Give as God gives. Love as God loves. And you will know your true self.

♡

May you rest in God's grace until the morning glory kisses your face.

♡

There is a stillness so serene and so pure, that words cannot describe it. This stillness was before any thought. This stillness was before time and space. This stillness always was and always will be. This stillness is infinite. This stillness simply IS. This stillness is your divine self. This stillness is what you are searching for. In the stillness of the holy instant, you will know God.

You can only feel uncomfortable around other people if you are uncertain about who you are, and who your brothers and sisters are. Uncomfortable feelings are only there because you believe that you are alone and separated. When you realize that you are One with your brothers and sisters, all uncomfortable feelings will disappear. You will have stepped into your certainty — your true self. One with all and One with God.

♡

Everything you want to feel, you need to extend from within you. If you want to feel kindness, be kind. If you want to feel love, be loving. If you want to feel peace, then be the peace that you want to feel. It all begins with YOU!!!

♡

Anything you identify with will seemingly limit you. As long as you hold on to any roles and concepts, you will not experience consistent peace and eternal love. Roles and concepts block the awareness of the light that you are.
By letting go of what you are not, you will remember who you are.

♡

Prayer is an act that is beyond the body. It is a divine communication tool to reach God directly. It doesn't need words. Prayer is not dependent on time or place. True prayer is from the heart. It leaps you into eternity and brings you directly to God the instant you pray to Him. Prayer is a way to remember the truth — because when you pray you are making an act to connect with Oneness, instead of holding on to a belief in separation. True prayer is for remembering that you are loved, and that you are love itself. True prayer is not for getting anything. It is for the remembrance of who you are. A divine being is in need of nothing. Prayer brings you to the Kingdom of Heaven within. It humbles your heart and washes away pride. It is a gateway to eternity.
Prayer brings you to Heaven. It brings you Home.

♡

*By quieting your mind, you will open your heart.
A mind free from obstacles to love's presence knows true love.*

♡

*Any problem you perceive in the world is in your mind. If you perceive a problem in a brother, the problem is in your mind. Absolutely everything you perceive is in your mind. It is all in your mind. The only solution to any perceived problem is to go within and see the core issue. The core issue is always the same belief; the belief that you are separated from God and from your brothers. This can be tricky, but this is the journey to awakening from the dream of illusions. At some point on the journey, you will see no separation, but only perceive Oneness — and your mind will be in a state of bliss. There is no problem out there and the perceived problem has already been corrected, as it simply was a mistaken belief in the mind. There never really was any problem!
You are whole and One with God right now.
It is all complete — and it always was.*

Prayer is a way to true humility.

♡

Eventually, you will need to face your deepest fears. There is no escaping from it, if you truly desire to awaken. To realize your true self, you will need to let go of everything that seems to be blocking you from the light of truth — and that is fear in seemingly different forms. You are free though, to wait with your self-realization until the next lifetime, or wait hundreds — or even thousands of lifetimes, but it is completely unnecessary to wait. Time is an illusion, so waiting is a trick. Waking up is inevitable and the only time there is is now! Now is the time to awaken from the dream of illusions! It does take willingness, devotion and unwavering commitment to walk through the darkness and into the light. Remember that thousands of angels are lighting the way for you, and Jesus is holding your hand. Trust this is so, and you will realize that you are the light that you are trying to find in the darkness. Fear is simply just imagined. Don't be afraid to look at it. It is not who you are. The fear of the fear is what is seemingly keeping you from looking at it, and letting it go. It's all just a trick to cover over the truth. The truth is that you are the light of the world.

AN AFTERTHOUGHT

I Am All There Is

Love Is

All I Am Is Love

♡

RESOURCES

Resources by Svava Kristin Love

Music:
https://store.livingmiracles.org

Divine Essence

The Light of Truth

Grace of God

Podcast Channels:

https://www.spreaker.com/show/into-the-mystic-with-svava-love

https://www.spreaker.com/show/the-mystical-divine-with-svava-love

Artist Channel:

https://www.youtube.com/@svavakristinlove

Books by Living Miracles Publications and David Hoffmeister:

This Moment Is Your Miracle

The Mystical Teachings of Jesus

Awakening through A Course in Miracles

The Movie Watcher's Guide to Enlightenment

Quantum Forgiveness: Physics, Meet Jesus

Unwind Your Mind Back to God: Experiencing A Course in Miracles

Jesus: A Gospel of Love

Available in print, eBook, and audiobook formats. Select materials available in thirteen languages.

Online Resources of David Hoffmeister and Living Miracles:

https://davidhoffmeister.com
A website about David Hoffmeister and his Teachings

https://www.youtube.com/user/DavidHoffmeister
Teachings by David on his YouTube Channel

https://www.spreaker.com/show/the_david_hoffmeister_show
The latest audio talks by David Hoffmeister

https://www.livingmiracles.org
Learn more about the Living Miracles Community

https://store.livingmiracles.org
David Hoffmeister Books and Resources

https://www.the-christ.net/
Practice and Living the Mystical Teachings of Jesus

https://mwge.org
Online Portal to Movies for Awakening

https://acim.me
Searchable Audios by David Hoffmeister

https://levelsofmind.org
The Levels of Mind Instrument and the Fast Track to Peace

https://acourseinmiraclesnow.org
Read *A Course in Miracles* Online

www.ingramcontent.com/pod-product-compliance
Lightning Source LLC
Chambersburg PA
CBHW061757070526
44586CB00023B/2615